BRILLIANT BUDGETS

AND

DESPICABLE DEBT

Book 1: $mall Change-Big Reward$

HEIDI FARRELLY

Edited by Elaine Roughton

Cover art by suhadiyono94

Cover design by mnsartstudionew

To my amazing mum, who always put food on the table and clothes on our backs no matter how much money was in her pocket. Thank you for always putting us first mum.

I love you xx

CONTENTS

INTRODUCTION

If you have ever tried and failed at budgeting, if you want to take charge of your debt and create cohesive goals for your future, and if you want to achieve the milestones you set out to reach in life, then you *need* to read this book. It will change the way you view your finances, and will create a firm groundwork on which to supercharge your future.

It doesn't matter if you don't have time or knowledge. It makes no difference if you hate budgets, or love them, or if you just want to reach a small goal. It doesn't matter if you suck at math or are neck deep in debt. *Brilliant Budgets and Despicable Debt* has something for everyone, whatever your situation.

You've already demonstrated a willingness to change by picking up this book, but it's up to you whether you do anything with the knowledge it contains. Budgets are incredibly personal and have to be driven from within. Only you can create a budget that satisfies your needs. Just like starting a diet, budgeting can be hard, but the longer you do it, the easier it becomes, until it's just as much a part of you as breathing. You just have to start.

Brilliant Budgets and Despicable Debt will walk you through multiple ways to budget, including how to NOT budget and still save money, how to budget while still living a life you love, and most importantly, how to incorporate a budget into your life so it becomes, not a time sucking burden, but a true resource.

We talk about how a good budget can help you pay off debt - no matter how deep you're in - and how to stay out of debt forever! The humble budget is truly one of the most important things you can master in your financial life.

How important? My husband and I are set to pay off our Sydney mortgage in just 10 years. Not through any great windfall or inheritance, but from being wise with the money we earnt, making cuts where we could, and finding contentment in the things life offered us instead of those we didn't have.

Budgeting alone will save us hundreds of thousands of dollars in loan interest. I mean hundreds of thousands! It doesn't get more real than that! And none of it would have been achievable if we hadn't started with a great budget.

Budgets are not a quick fix, a magic solution that creates more wealth from the same income, but they *are* a way of ensuring the income you make goes towards the things you want it to, rather than being frittered away. Budgets are perfect if you want to stop:

- Wondering where your money goes each week
- Fighting about money
- Worrying about money
- Going into debt each month
- Making excuses about your money
- Dreaming about things, instead of doing them

Yes, budgets take time, but how much time do you spend worrying about money? Do you spend hours dreaming about holidays, house renovations, or freedom from debt? I know I do. However, I dream about them with a plan in mind, and I know that over time I'll make my dreams a reality. Are you so certain?

If you want to travel, have financial freedom, own a holiday home, or simply live without money worries, then let this comprehensive book make your dreams a reality. Don't let a perceived lack of time or understanding strip you of all the benefits a great budget can provide.

The sooner you start, the sooner you'll begin realising your dreams. Because dreams only become reality when action is taken.

Let's kick off with *Chapter 1: What Are Budgets and Why Should I Use Them? Aren't They an Old Person Thing?* It runs through exactly what a budget is and is not, and helps you understand how they can be used to improve every area of your life. Are you ready to do more than just dream?

CHAPTER 1:
WHAT ARE BUDGETS AND WHY SHOULD I USE THEM? AREN'T THEY AN OLD PERSON THING?

Why do people have so much trouble with budgeting? It's a relatively simple exercise, and the Internet is littered with self-help guides, graphs, and how-tos. Have you tried budgeting before, but never made it past the first month? Or reached your first goal and then felt the enthusiasm start to wane, and then disappear altogether? So why do we all struggle so much?

I know for me, it was because I always wrote the budget I wanted, rather than the one that worked. Others miscalculate their ongoing costs, or income, and for some people the endless money watching and calculations simply drive them mad, and they give up before their shiny new budgets ever had a chance to work.

Budgeting is seen by many as something that only old people do. And you'd be right.

But look at those same 'old people' and you'll see they are in a much better financial state than most of us. And yes, a lot of that was due to the era they grew up in, but they were also a lot more conscious of their money. They made do and they did without, if they didn't have enough money that week. They were taught to keep a weekly account of their spending. How many of us can say the same?

Before virtual wallets and online banking, before credit cards and pay wave, before calculators and apps, money was a much simpler animal to understand. You got your wages, and they went towards paying a mortgage, putting food on the table, and gas in your car, and if you were lucky there was money left over for treats, holidays, and saving.

The only loans people really had were their mortgages, and later on maybe a car loan. Student loans, credit cards, and direct debits just didn't exist. If you didn't have it, you couldn't spend it. It was this, as well as a greater awareness of where their money went, that allowed our grandparents to pay off their homes, save for goals, and generally keep track of their spending.

Sadly, it is now only too easy to get into strife when it comes to money. If we don't have enough one week, we just chuck it on the credit card. Keeping a weekly tally of spending is seemingly only done by anally retentive weirdos, and even if we wanted to budget, most people would have no idea where to start.

It's not like budgeting is part of the school curriculum or anything. Looking after your money just isn't taught, and isn't seen as important. But why not? Creating a great budget is the single most important thing you can do to help you achieve your goals, and create a future you'll love for yourself. Your budget will tell you:

- What your combined income sources are
- What you spend your money on
- How much you have left at the end of every week
- Any areas you can cut costs in
- How much you can afford to save
- How fast you can pay off your debt and get ahead
- How you can achieve your savings goals sooner

Put simply, budgets are a way of looking at your money with a new perspective. Done right, they become a snapshot of everything you have spent your money on in the past, and what you plan to spend your money on in the future. You can see your total expenditure in relation to your income, where you spend the most money, and any areas that would benefit from a fresh look.

You'll probably learn more about your spending habits than you care to know… If you're struggling with debt, and are swamped with credit card bills and loan repayments, then a good budget can show you the way out. But knowing how to budget is not enough. Being able to sustain that budget is far more important.

Do you want to know if you'll ever be able to afford that holiday, car, or house? A budget can do this. Do you want to get out of debt as quickly as possible and start saving your money instead? A budget can help you with this too. Or are you simply curious about where your hard-earned cash vanishes to each week? Budget, budget, budget!

I mean seriously, why wouldn't you write and follow a budget if it can give you all these things? We go over all the common excuses in *Chapter 2*, but it's pretty simple. Budgeting takes time, knowledge, and a willingness to change. And people just don't think it's worth their while. Let's face it: nobody likes to hear the word 'budget.' It's up there with 'diet' in the dirty word stakes, but the reality is, if you don't know what you spend your money on, you just can't get ahead.

My bestselling book *Mortgage Free*[1] tackles budgeting as its very first chapter. Why? Because before you can get rid of debt and pay off a home loan, you have to know not only how much you make, but how much you're holding onto. It's this knowledge that allows you to build a sustainable budget that truly works for you, and helps you build a foundation for your future plans and goals.

---

[1] http://amzn.to/1NBMTKQ

My dreams haven't always come true. I used to spend hours on Facebook looking at other peoples' holidays and wishing I could afford to do the same. It wasn't until I started taking charge of my finances that I realised I could! I just needed to use my time and money more wisely, and the world opened up!

You can gain the knowledge you need to begin budgeting and tackle debt, just by reading this book. You may not get it right the first time, but neither did I! I spent years struggling with crappy budgets, but I'm now so good at them that I'm able to help others with theirs.

You don't have to spend years. *Brilliant Budgets and Despicable Debt* will help you choose a budget that suits you and your lifestyle, and eliminate all the ones that don't. Talk about getting a leg up!

If you are short of money, there are only really two options available to you. Make more, or save more. And if you make more, are you guaranteed to save more? No. Because the reality is, when we make more, we spend more. Budgets provide a kind of early warning system that can alert you when something is going wrong, and allow you to make changes for the better, no matter what you're earning.

Budgeting is more essential now than it ever has been before. So regardless of which budget you choose, and how well you do, know that any step towards a better understanding of your money, and how you spend it, is a step forward.

Recap:

- Budgeting is applicable to people of any age and in any financial situation
- Budgeting is less understood now than ever before, but is not hard to learn or implement
- Creating a budget is the single most important thing you can do to help you understand and grow your finances

- Budgeting takes time, knowledge, and a willingness to change

Download the free worksheet[2] for help identifying why you want to budget, and your feelings on them.

Find out more about what time, knowledge, and emotion have to do with budgeting, and how we can challenge our mindsets to create a budget that actually works in *Chapter 2: Why People Don't Budget: Confronting Mindsets and Beliefs*. Which excuse is holding you back?

---

[2] http://www.how2without.com/bonus-materials/bbdd-pdf-workbook/

CHAPTER 2:

WHY PEOPLE DON'T BUDGET: CONFRONTING MINDSETS AND BELIEFS

There are many reasons people don't budget, but they all come back to 3 base points. TIME (takes too long), KNOWLEDGE (lack of, or misunderstanding), and EMOTION (attachment to money, freedom of use, resistance to change).

Below, I've listed some of the main reasons people give for not budgeting, and the solution to each problem. I have tried to illustrate each point honestly, and with as little fluff as possible.

Problem: *Budgets are too restrictive. They don't allow me to do what I normally do with my money. I hate feeling controlled (emotion).*

Solution: Budgets do not have to be this way. The reason a budget is restrictive is because you have not given yourself enough 'wiggle room.' Every budget is as individual as the person using it, and no one budget will suit everyone. If it feels restrictive, then it is not a good fit. Pick one that fits your needs, not your ideals. A budget done well can be very liberating.

Problem: *Budgets are depressing. Spending money is not called retail therapy for nothing. There is an emotional high that comes with spending (as well as cool stuff) and I don't want to give that up (emotion).*

Solution: Budgets are depressing because people try to restrict their spending too much. You should always have money for spending on things you want just for the sake of wanting them. Most diets fail because they ask people to give up all the foods they really enjoy, and bad budgets are the same. If you have to give up all the fun stuff, something is wrong.

Problem: *I don't want to know how much I'm spending. It just makes me feel guilty, or compelled to make changes I don't want to make. Ignorance is bliss! (emotion)*

Solution: And if you have bucket loads of money this might be okay, but I suspect you're reading a budgeting book for a reason... Even if money is not an issue now, your future may not be so rosy. Do you know what all leading businesses have in common? They all have oodles of money and they all have budgets. Every one of them.

Because without knowing what they spend their money on, they cannot effectively plan, grow, or develop. And the same is true of individuals. Knowing what you spend your money on today is vital to how you can grow your money for the future.

Problem: *Budgets are time consuming, and I always have to adjust them. (time).*

Solution: Budgeting can be time consuming, especially at the beginning when you are learning what works and what doesn't. However, I find this is counterbalanced by spending less time worrying about how you can afford that bill, those school uniforms, or simply this week's rent.

With a budget, you already know how much you have, where you can make cuts in emergencies, and how much you need every week to survive. While you may make small changes now and then, a good budget should not constantly need work. If it does, then you may need to reassess which budget type suits you best.

Problem: *Budgets are confusing. I can't wrap my head around how they work, and how they can work for me (knowledge).*

Solution: Budgeting does not have to be confusing, and yet they often become so because people create intricate budgets that are akin to a cryptic crossword! This is not necessary, and just adds to peoples' confusion, and increases the speed with which they give up altogether.

People have this belief that the budget that is working 'for everyone else' should work for them too. When it doesn't, they think the problem is with how they have set the budget up, or that they have done something wrong, adding to the confusion. In reality, they have probably just picked a budget that doesn't suit them.

The old adage of 'Keep it simple, stupid' (K.I.S.S) is definitely true of budgets. They don't have to be intricate and they don't have to be confusing. Simply put, budgets work by showing you how much you spend and what you spend your money on. They can help you reduce costs, start saving, and be more conscious of how your money is being used each week. Even if you choose a non-budget! Simple, not confusing.

Problem: *I don't even break even most weeks, let alone have money left over. My situation is too bad for a budget to work (knowledge).*

Solution: If you are struggling to make ends meet, then you probably need a budget even more than someone who is looking to save money through budgeting. Budgets are not just a tool to help people who have money; their most useful job is actually to show people where they are spending their money and how they can minimize this spending.

It highlights the areas that you can work on, and those that are already succeeding. To be always treading water, and living paycheck-to-paycheck sucks big time, but a good budget can ensure there is nothing slipping through the cracks, and that the money you have gets spent in the best way possible.

A quick note, however. In some countries, including the United States, there are people who are not even earning a 'living wage.' This means that what they earn doesn't cover their living expenses - rent, food, and utilities. It doesn't matter how hard they work, they just can't get ahead.

For example: The minimum wage in the USA is $7.25 an hour. New Zealand's minimum wage, on the other hand, is increasing in 2016 to $15.25 an hour. Over double that of the USA. Include the fact that NZ has free hospital care, workers' compensation, and plenty of jobs, and you have a huge difference in people's ability to get ahead.

If this sounds like a situation you know only too well, then I would encourage you to use your budget to *assess* your situation. Figure out what you're currently spending, how much you need to survive, and how much extra it would take to start getting ahead. Use what will probably be a negative dollar amount as your goal, and then work out how to make it a reality.

My book *Mortgage Free*[3] has lots of ideas on earning extra income. Read it, and see if you can use any of them to your advantage. There are also some fabulous books available on Amazon about side incomes or side hustles. I've listed the best ones on my site[4]. They cover how to work smarter, not harder, and how to bring in a side income that will supplement your wage.

Problem: *I earn more than enough money and don't need a budget (knowledge).*

Solution: A budget does not have to be instituted when you're broke. In fact, if you can implement a budget while you're still flush, you may find you never get to that point. A budget helps you understand your spending and your saving habits, and encourages you to be mindful of what's coming in and what's going out.

---

[3] http://amzn.to/1NBMTKQ

[4] http://www.how2without.com/bonus-materials/bbdd-pdf-workbook/

Often people with 'plenty of money' find that they are actually spending more every month because 'they can afford it.' What happens when you can't? If you lose your job, or have a child, or simply start spending more than you make, will your mind automatically convert to 'I can't afford it now?'

No, probably not. Because you're not even thinking about your money. Budgeting is not necessarily the suspension of spending, it is just having knowledge of where your money is going. Do you know where yours is being spent?

Problem: *I'm unsure how to create and use a budget (knowledge).*

Solution: With all the spreadsheets, apps, and printable forms on the Internet, budgeting has never been easier. But while the tools for budgeting are readily available, often the knowledge on how to set one up successfully, and stick to it, is not. It is not hard to learn though, and the time you invest in doing so will be repaid tenfold in the benefits a good budget brings. I will give you a step by step guide on how to budget throughout this book.

Problem: *Budgeting doesn't give me a plan or a goal, there is no sense of achievement or purpose (emotion).*

Solution: The number 1 mistake people make with their budget, is not connecting it to a plan or a goal. Your goal might be as simple as finding out what you spend your money on, or as complex as saving money for 10 different things, but you always need a goal. Without one, your budget becomes just another mindless chore, rather than a tool for success.

I am very goal oriented, and knowing I am saving money is not enough. I have to have a final figure, or a travel destination in mind - something to encourage me and remind me what I'm aiming for. Planning and goal setting are two fantastic and ridiculously easy ways to encourage you and help ensure success.

Problem: *I live for today - I don't want to always plan for the future (knowledge and time).*

Solution: Living in the moment is awesome, and something I always try to do. But you can still live today and prepare for tomorrow. What happens when the future is not as rosy as today? With a bit of planning, if things do go south, it is less noticeable and far more manageable if you have a plan in place, and takes far less time than you think.

There are ways to budget without even budgeting (see *Chapter 9*) and they will not stop you living your life to the max. I know, because my life is full, and exciting, and I don't spend much time on budgeting. I just spend enough to ensure my future is as rosy (or even rosier), than my present.

Problem: *You have to be good at math to budget - I'm not (knowledge).*

Solution: Some people create budgets that need mathematicians to work them out, but the simplest budgets are often the best ones. You don't have to be great at math. You don't even have to be good at math! Budgets are about knowledge, not math. Yes, that knowledge is of your money, and money is linked with math, but there doesn't need to be complex calculations or mass arithmetic happening.

In fact, with online calculators, apps that do all the work for you, and budgets that aren't budgets, you should be able to find a solution that suits you. Check out some of the budgets we have collected further on, and you'll soon see you don't need a math degree for any of them.

Problem: *Predicting my earning and spending is too hard (knowledge and time).*

Solution: If you don't have a steady income, or if your spending changes every week, then budgeting can seem like a colossal nightmare! But it doesn't have to be. Most budgets start with the assumption that people know what they're spending, and earning, but this is not the case for almost anyone. Do we really know what we're earning or where all our money goes? Don't stress though, *Chapter 3* will give you the tools you need to combat this so it's no longer a problem.

Recap:

- Time, knowledge, and emotion are the main reasons people don't budget.
- Budgets do not have to be restrictive or depressing.
- Knowledge of what you spend today can mean your future is a lot more certain.
- You don't have to be good at math to budget.
- You don't have to have a regular income or even regular spending habits to create a usable budget.
- Budgets can work for anyone. It doesn't matter if you have oodles of money, or none.
- Budgets are a lot easier to create and use than most people think.
- Planning and goal setting are two fantastic and ridiculously easy ways to encourage you and help ensure success.

Hopefully this answers the most common questions and concerns you may have about budgeting. You can download a worksheet that helps you address these problems[5] but if you have any more queries, please

---

[5] http://www.how2without.com/bonus-materials/bbdd-pdf-workbook/

feel free to reach out to me on Facebook[6] or on Twitter[7]. I'd be happy to help you out.

Up next, we take on *Chapter 3: Why Most Budgets Fail and How to Make Yours Work Even If You Suck at Budgeting.* If you've ever tried and failed at budgeting, then this will be a must read!

---

[6] https://www.facebook.com/how2without/

[7] http://twitter.com/Heidi2233

CHAPTER 3:
WHY MOST BUDGETS FAIL AND HOW TO MAKE YOURS WORK EVEN IF YOU SUCK AT BUDGETING

I have always loved the *idea* of budgeting, but I never aced it until I was in my late 20's. So neatly laid out, and showing promise for savings and minimized spending, budgets were like making to-do lists, but with numbers. I wrote so many different budgets every year, and every one of them failed miserably!

Why? Because I always wrote the budget I *wanted* to have, the one with savings, and spending money, and money for holidays and cafés, with less spent on groceries and petrol. I never once stopped to think about what I already spent money on, short of the big ticket items and regular bills.

The key to budgets is spending less than you make. And the key to paying off debt, is saving more than you spend.

Doesn't sound hard, right? And yet, how many of us know what we're spending our money on? Sounds weird, I know! It's your money - of course you know what you're spending it on. But in reality, you probably only have an idea, rather than a firm grasp of your spending habits, and this is why most budgets fail. They assume you know where your money is going.

If you've read my first book, *Mortgage Free*[8], you may know how to complete the 10 steps below and collate your finance data ready for budgeting. Feel free to skip this chapter and start with *Chapter 4:*

[8] http://amzn.to/1NBMTKQ

Despicable Debt and its Dangerous Deeds. If you haven't read *Mortgage Free*, then read on and follow the 10 steps below BEFORE you try to create a budget for yourself. Believe me when I say it will be worth your while!

You are the *only* person who knows what you spend money on, your indulgences, your ongoing expenses, and the things that are important to you. There is no single budget that is the same as another. When you write a budget, there is no point writing something you would *like* to have, you have to make one that is sustainable, not just for a few months, but for the duration of your goals.

There are a million budget spreadsheets on the Internet, and the thing they all do in common is the very thing that is guaranteed to make them fail.

You write in how much you earn, followed by what you spend on big things such as rent, utilities, bills, food, etc., and what you have left over is your 'excess.' Pretty simple, right?

And if you are a monk, living in the middle of nowhere, who has no friends to buy presents for, no weddings to attend, no Christmas' to splurge on, and no pubs to crawl, then you'd probably be sweet! But if you are a little bit more normal than our friend the monk - it just ain't gonna work!

The elephant in the room here is that all those big bills you've written in, they only make up a portion of your life, and as such, you are only getting a snapshot of your spending. No matter how bad, you have to know what you're spending before you'll know what you can save.

So where is your money going? To know this, I mean to *truly* know this, you'll need to dedicate a bit of your time to finding out. In fact, this part of budgeting is perhaps the most labour intensive of the whole process. But it's also the most important. Do *not* skip these 10 steps!

They will make whichever budget you choose a breeze to implement and succeed at.

1. Write a budget the way you would like it to look.

You know those Internet spreadsheets that don't work? Yeah, grab one of those and fill it out. If you're not sure what I mean, download one[9].

Include how much you would like to spend on each item, keeping how much you earn in mind, and make sure to include how much you would like to save. Now put it away out of sight for a month. Not in one of those safe places where you'll never find again - you need it later.

2. Find something to record on.

This could be a notebook and pen, the 'notes' function on your phone, a draft email you can open from phone, iPad, or computer, a Word doc, an app – whatever, just make sure it is always accessible.

3. Write down EVERYTHING you spend.

I don't just mean the bills and the present you bought your mum. I mean the change you put in the parking meter, the school excursion you paid for in gold coins, the round at the pub, the coffee on the way to work, and the other coffee you *didn't* buy on your lunch break. EVERYTHING.

Don't forget to include your monthly, quarterly, and yearly bills like car insurance, power and water bills, mobile phone and Internet use, property rates, health insurance, etc., and the 5 debt baddies below.

- Student loans (include interest payments).
- Personal loans (include interest payments).

---

[9] www.how2without.com/

- Credit cards (include estimated interest payments).
- Interest-free finance (when do you start paying interest again and how much will it be?).
- Ongoing memberships and direct debits - include everything from gyms and lessons to Netflix and Spotify.

All these things need to be included in your budget.

I know it seems like a lot, but believe me, when you succeed at meeting every one of your goals, it will have been worth it! There are many apps that can help you simplify this process, by linking to your bank accounts and recording expenses and allowing you to scan in cash receipts. See *Chapter 10* for more details on these.

4. Do this for 4 weeks.

Is this a massive pain in the butt? Yes. Of course it is. Why would I pretend otherwise? But this is also the best groundwork you can do before creating a budget. If you can't even stick to writing down your spending for 4 weeks, there is no way in hell you're gonna be able to stick to the months or years needed to meet your goals, so dry your eyes and get writing.

5. Collate your data.

At the end of 4 weeks, sit down and collate all your data. Make yourself a spreadsheet or print ours,[10] and sort all your spending into groups.

---

[10] http://www.how2without.com/bonus-materials/bbdd-pdf-workbook/

Collate Your Spending Data

	Weekly	Monthly
Direct debits (subscriptions/donations/regular bills)	$145	$628
Groceries and Eating out (lunch/dinner/alcohol/coffee)	$282	$1,222
Going out (movies/holidays/nightlife/day trips)	$170	$740
Regular payment (car/phone/swimming lessons/spotify subscription)	$186	$810
Odds and Ends (parking/donations/school costs)	$23	$99
Bills (power/water/rates/insurance)	$134	$583
Retail therapy (clothes/electronics/shoes/music)	$108	$468
Transport (bus/train/petrol/gas)	$79	$342
Savings (retirement/tax/travel/debt)	$200	$866
Total Income	$1,100	$4767
Total Spend	$1,327	$5758
Remainder (+ or -)	-$227	-$991

6. Get your totals.

This is the scary part. Finding out how much you actually spend on things you don't really need and never knew you wanted…

Subtract this from what you earn and what you have left is your free money. If you have anything left. A lot of people find that although they are earning good money and not spending what they think is a lot, by the time they add in all the incidentals and day-to-day expenses they are running at a loss. See *Chapter 5* on credit card and other forms of debt.

7. Find that monk budget you put in a safe place.

Remember that crappy spreadsheet budget you wrote, the perfect one that would never work? Grab it out and compare it to your real life one. Go over all the differences and write them down as shown in the example.

Your reality is usually going to be somewhere in the middle of each of the two figures. Sometimes you'll find they line up, (if you're lucky), and other times there is just no way the two will ever be friends. Check out the graph below. It is a perfect example of how cutting back in some areas can give you a lot more money where it counts - without cramping your style!

Remember that the 'real budget' is based on how you spend now. The 'monk budget' was the perfect spreadsheet budget you filled out, and the 'true budget' is your middle ground - what you're aiming for. As you can see, with a little bit of trimming you end up with a tidy savings amount each week, without making other areas unsustainable. Print off a fillable true budget form to help you get started[11].

---

[11] http://www.how2without.com/bonus-materials/bbdd-pdf-workbook/

REAL - MONK - TRUE - BUDGET COMPARISON

	REAL BUDGET	MONK BUDGET	TRUE BUDGET
Mortgage/Rent	$400	$400	$400
Groceries	$180	$100	$150
Petrol	$120	$70	$100
Bills	$250	$150	$200
Spending	$150	$50	$50
Savings	$0	$330	$200
TOTAL	$1,100	$1,100	$1,100

8. Trim.

This is the hardest part of budgeting and the part people suck at the most. Sit down with your partner or your imaginary friend and really look at your spending. See where you can make cuts, save money, and dial back.

9. Stick at it!

Okay, so maybe this is the hardest part of budgeting. Sometimes the changes you make just don't work, and other times they are a lot easier than you imagined. A lot of it is trial and error; the important thing is to have a goal and stick to it. If you spent more in one area this week, it has to come from somewhere, and it can't be your credit card, so another area has to suffer.

10. Nothing is forever. Review and re-work.

Everything changes over time. Children are born, cars break down, jobs are lost and gained, and life interferes in a million different ways.

Your budget therefore changes too. HOWEVER, how much you put into your savings account or into achieving your goals shouldn't change if you want to reach them in this lifetime.

As soon as you start cutting a little bit one week, it becomes a slippery slope into doing it every week, until you whittle that little bit of extra down to a whole lot of nothing. This means that when you originally write your budget, you have to be absolutely certain you are putting away an amount that is sustainable in the long term, no matter what crops up.

Over time you may find a bit of non-essential spending creeping back into your carefully worked budget. Don't be afraid to take another look at it whenever needed and see what might have changed.

Bills normally increase every year, and supposedly so do our wages, although this can be a bit of a joke. You will probably need to re-write your budget occasionally, but be sure you are still saving money for your goals, whether that's paying off debt, saving for a holiday or for your retirement, and leaving yourself enough to live on.

Recap:

- A good budget is vital to your success, but most don't take into account those everyday expenses that really add up.
- Make certain you include ALL your expenses when budgeting.
- Use apps to help you catalogue your bills and expenses
- Review your budget periodically, ensuring it is still working with you and your life.

Once you've mastered these 10 steps, set your sights on where you want to be in the future. Don't forget you can download all the worksheets to help complete these steps for free on our website[12].

Now that you know what you're spending, let me introduce you to Despicable Debt. Or are you already acquainted? Find out in *Chapter 4: Despicable Debt and its Dangerous Deeds.*

[12] http://www.how2without.com/bonus-materials/bbdd-pdf-workbook/

CHAPTER 4:
DESPICABLE DEBT AND ITS DANGEROUS DEEDS

Despicable, really? Isn't that a bit over the top? Maybe. How about we try some other words? All consuming. Pervasive. Soul sucking. Destroyer of life, of love, of relationships, of families.

Debt is truly one of the ugliest words I know. However you see it, or say it, debt can be the difference between a life well lived, and a life not lived at all.

People see it as a necessary evil, and it has become such an accepted part of our society that its tendrils can be found in many forms, in every age group, and in every walk of life.

And yet we can't wait to be free of it. Somewhere in our psyche (pushed deep down where we don't have to think about it often), we know that debt is *not* a necessary evil, but just an evil. I've seen debt destroy relationships, happiness, and lives, and it's heartbreaking.

It's also unnecessary.

Yes, some things are nearly impossible without debt (think mortgages), but most other forms of debt are *avoidable* and *preventable*. You just need the knowledge and the willpower to walk that path.

In our grandparents' day there wasn't nearly so much debt. The cost of living helped enormously. But it wasn't just that. Our elders were brought up when things like credit cards didn't exist and there weren't loans to fall back on. They knew that if they didn't have the money they couldn't buy it.

But somewhere along the line we have lost what is possibly one of the most important lessons you can learn in life! It seems so simple. If you don't have the money, don't buy it. And yet, people everywhere have turned this common sense piece of advice on its head and it has become instead, "I can't afford it now so I will just put it on credit and pay it when I can."

What the hell! When did buying something with non-existent money become okay? When did it stop being frowned upon? When did people start talking with pride about the car they bought on finance, the holiday they got a loan for, or the dress they whacked on their credit card?

Society has a lot to answer for. Advertising pushes the "must have" lounge suite, the "affordable" new car, and the "interest free" credit cards. There is an expectation that to be successful you must "have," and to have, you have to spend, whether you've got the money or not.

People feel they need to have the big house, the fast car, and the labelled clothing right off the bat. There is no waiting for anything. It is an instantaneous life. Why save when you could get it now?

You see co-workers who always seem to have the latest and greatest kitchen appliances, boats, and beach houses, and know they are on a similar wage. If they have it all, why can't you?

But what you don't see is their debt. That skulking, insidious bedfellow that lurks beneath everything they do. Credit cards are maxed, they're mortgaged to the hilt, and they're struggling. Maybe not on the surface. Instagram posts are still rosy, and they're still stepping out in their Jimmy Choos, but behind closed doors they sit with their bills and worry.

And yet, nothing changes. They continue to spend, and their debt continues to grow. These people will never know the freedom of being debt free, and will never understand the joy that can be gained by living life without the weight of debt.

Sadly, I think people use this uncontrolled spending as an excuse for not getting ahead. "I can't afford to travel or buy a house." "It's not my fault." "I just don't earn enough." "How can I ever save a deposit?"

How? Start at the bottom like your parents and their parents before them.

Yes, they have lovely houses and new cars now. They lunch out and travel when they like. But this wasn't always the way. Before the lovely house was probably a crappy one, before the new car, an old one. Before they ate out, they packed lunches, and picnics, and camped close to home instead of flying overseas.

They didn't expect to have everything the day they started working and society didn't expect it of them either.

But it's not all society's fault! People are individuals, not lemmings, and we are free to make our own choices in life. Our generation is the first to think it's okay not to work if there isn't a job available in our field of expertise, to buy what they want instead of what they can afford, and it is starting to show.

Our parents' generation took whatever jobs were available. They weren't too good to stack shelves, do manual labour, or work beneath bosses they hated. They didn't mind starting with what they could afford and working their way up to what they wanted! That's just the way it was. And it is this mentality that saw them succeed, live lower stress lives, and get joy out of the little things!

People were more resourceful. They made things, they made do, and they did things themselves. More of their paycheck stayed in their pockets because of this.

It's not rocket science, people! If you don't have it, don't spend it!

Of course this is all just a broad generalisation of the decades, but debt is a little like the devil. If it doesn't get you one way, you can bet your bottom dollar it will try another route.

Like Gloria Gaynor sings in 'I Will Survive,' despicable debt is like a dodgy boyfriend. It keeps on coming back. So how do we combat it? If we're in it, how do we get out? And how do we stop it getting back in? Hang tight, we're going to address that next.

Sing it with me now. "I should have changed those stupid locks, I should have made you leave your key, if I thought for just one second you'd be back to bother me! Whoa whoa."

So what is debt?

Debt is any expense that you currently owe in your life. For anything.

When you are looking at buying a house, getting a credit card, or applying for a loan, the first thing the banks look at is all of your current outgoings — your debt and your bills. This includes (but is certainly not limited to), college degrees, "interest-free" finance for cars, furniture, and holidays, Lay-By, credit cards, data plans for phones and tablets, personal loans, not to mention your day-to-day bills and expenses. The list is endless.

They affect how much you can borrow, how fast you can pay back your loan, and your ability to save, and pay off debt.

The biggest forms of debt (other than mortgages) are:

1. Credit cards
2. Personal loans
3. Student loans

4. Monthly direct debits for memberships and subscriptions
5. Interest-free finance deals

All of these count against you when you're applying for anything bank related. Want to start a new business? Banks will hesitate to advance you money if you're already in debt, and likewise investors will be cautious to shell out their hard earned cash, as they can't see anything except the hole you're already in.

Buying a house? All your outgoings will dictate how much you can borrow. Not only this, but having previous debt severely limits your ability to save, and pay off your new form of debt. It's a vicious cycle that is incredibly hard to escape from.

Even if you aren't trying to get a loan or prove yourself to a bank, debt plays a huge role in how you live your life. From being able to afford a holiday, to buying a new outfit, to giving your kids lessons in something they love. All of these things become so much more achievable without the burden of debt.

If you could wipe every scrap of debt that you currently have, mortgage, credit cards, finance and loans, and start from scratch; what would your life be like? Is the idea of having no debt like a fairy tale to you? Do you, like many people I know, believe you will never be out of debt, and that you might as well just keep on going the way you are?

There is always a way out. It might not be easy - in fact I can almost guarantee it won't be - but it is achievable and it is so worth it!

Recap:

- If you don't have it, don't spend it!
- Debt is much harder to escape today than ever before, but that doesn't mean it's completely unavoidable.

- Debt is anything you owe money on such as credit cards, personal loans, and memberships.
- Becoming debt free is not impossible, but requires hard work and dedication.

You're not going to like it, but up next is *Chapter 5 - The Devil is in the Details - and the Debt*, so buckle your seat belts and hang on for the ride, while we talk about credit cards and finance and the massive role they play in people's debt levels. And then I'm going to show you how to break free of debt and get rid of it once and for all.

CHAPTER 5:
THE DEVIL IS IN THE DETAILS – AND THE DEBT

A parallel universe - When debt can be good

Let's start with the good - sadly there's not much of it, so try not to get a false sense of security…

If you have never had a credit card, look at signing up for one. While always paying cash for everything is an admirable trait, it leaves you with no credit record. If you pay for everything on a credit card but pay the balance off each month, then companies are able to see your spending. This gives you a better credit rating than someone who doesn't use a credit card at all.

It's backwards, I know, but that's just the way the system works, and you have to roll with it.

Other types of 'good' debt are an investment property that is lowering your tax bracket or a small business that is running at a 'loss' even while staying afloat, due to being able to claim many things others can't at the end of the tax year.

There is a very fine line between good debt and bad though, so tread carefully. Okay, gird your loins and let's talk about credit cards.

Credit Cards

Credit cards are like a bottomless sinkhole from which there is no escape. And the good old banks have made them even more accessible now than ever before. Think of credit cards like a problem gambler. People know they shouldn't spend the money, they even make plans to cut them up, hide them, and keep away from the shops, but eventually they always cave.

How do I know? Because I was that person! When I was in my late teens and early twenties, I used credit cards to pay for 'just the things I really needed.' Only problem was, while I started off paying my one credit card down to zero every month, the debt slowly crept up until there was so much I despaired of ever paying it off.

Credit card debt doesn't always happen slowly, or through money mismanagement though. Sometimes life just smacks you in the face, and things like medical expenses take your credit card from zero to thousands in a split second.

Not everyone is as lucky as I am here in Australia. We have free healthcare and doctors, but I have friends in the US who pay hundreds to take their kids to emergency rooms, and thousands for necessary surgery. Instant debt. It's so sad.

Credit cards are also used to bridge the gap when things come up unexpectedly or when you lose your job, or health. While these things can't be helped, the end result is the same.

Now lucky for me, back then (erm… 15 years ago), credit cards had low limits. Mine was $5,000. I also only had one card. So while $5,000 was a lot of money, it was nothing compared to the money people owe now. The current figure for average credit card debt in America stands at a little over $15,000.

But let's think about this for a minute. Not everyone owns a credit card. Of those that do own credit cards, many owe just a little bit or nothing at all. So that means that some people have exorbitant credit card debt. I'm talking numbers like $50,000. House deposit figures. Travel around the world for years kind of figures.

If you think that you could never get to this point, then think again. Remember what I said about despicable debt? It is pervasive, and insidious, and like a monster under the bed it can creep up on you slowly, or jump up fast!

I'm not saying that it comes unannounced. There are always indications of our impending doom. But like a screaming child we've learnt to tune it out. (Or is that just me?)

So how do we learn to pay attention before it's too late? Or if you are already at the point of no return (there is always hope, take a deep breath), how do you get back to square 1?

My wakeup call came when we bought a house. Up until then I had been able to tell myself that 'with the next pay I'd knock off my credit card.' Sound familiar? Well, when I was faced with the fact that my next pay would be being spent on my mortgage, and the one after that, and the one after that… I realised I had to pull up my bootstraps.

I managed to knock off a couple of grand before the mortgage went through, but it still meant that I had $3,000 on my credit card. I will never forget the shame I felt when my husband realised I owed 3 grand.

I had a good job, we lived simply, and he had no debt. (He's always been amazing with money - sigh). We had separate accounts, so up until buying a house together, he had no reason to know where my credit card debt stood. Poor man probably just assumed I had none. Again - so ashamed.

He paid off my credit card and I paid him back slowly when I could. And that was the last time I ran up debt on my credit card. His disappointment was more than I could bear. And not only that. I had something concrete to work for. We wanted to pay off our home loan in 10 years, and I was committed to making that happen.

But what happens if you and your partner are both bad with money? Or if you've been bought up in a family where credit card debt is not something to be ashamed of? Or you just haven't hit that point yet where you know something needs to be done?

It is so, so easy just to exist. You know it's not right, you know you'll probably regret it in the long run, but for now it is easy. And now is where you're at. If this is you, living in the now, then I challenge you to do a 5-year snapshot of your future.

Five years isn't far off in the scheme of things. But if you take your debt levels now and multiply them by 5, you will start to realise that struggling in quicksand only makes you sink deeper. There is a step-by-step guide to doing a 5-year finance snapshot on my website[13]. It is not a download. It is free for you to access any time you need to.

Loans, Finance and other trouble makers

Okay, so if credit cards are like a problem gambler struggling in quicksand, what is the difference between them and loans?

Nothing. Not really. The only difference is that where credit card debt usually builds up slowly from 100 different things, loans and finance deals are mostly used for one or two big items. And in some ways this makes them worse.

Why? Because we see them as having more value. Of being worth more to us. Your money isn't being frittered away, and you have something big and tangible to show for it.

A house, a car, a college degree, a new sofa or kitchen or bathroom. Whatever it is, you can say, "I owe $50,000 but I am a dentist now and I can earn it back." Or, "I may be in debt, but I really needed a new car. It was worth it." But what is the real cost of that debt? Are

---

[13] http://www.how2without.com/finance-snapshot/

there other options? At first glance it may not seem like it, but look closer.

Student Loans

Could you have worked for a year and saved money for college instead of using a loan? In Australia and New Zealand this is plausible. We have a high minimum wage, and you can work your way through college, living frugally, and come out the other side with almost no debt.

In America and other countries around the world it is a very different story, but there are still options. Could you do an apprenticeship, get a scholarship, or do an internship? Could you take your course at night or over a longer period, allowing you to work part time and study part time? Could you do a cheaper course and build on it once you have been working for a few years?

Is the course you're doing something you truly love, or are you simply doing it because it's expected of you, or you don't know what else to do? So many students realise they don't enjoy a subject, or their job prospects are not what they expected, halfway through their degree.

They either end up dropping out and starting another course, which is a colossal waste of time and money, or they continue, and end up miserable in a job they hate. Be sure you are studying something you really want to do, and if you're not sure then don't rush into it!

I think the Brits definitely have the right way of doing things with their gap year. Not only does it give people a break between the end of high school and the beginning of university, it opens them up to new experiences, options, and ideas, and helps them understand what they really want out of life. Mark Twain had it right when he said:

"Broad, wholesome, charitable views of men and things cannot be acquired by vegetating in one little corner of the earth all one's lifetime."

You can work your way around the world too, seeing everything you want to and working as you go. This way you return home with no debt but having seen the world and found your place in it. More on that in another book…

If you do decide to go ahead with an expensive college degree, it just means you have to work harder at the other end to get rid of it. So be very sure to look at all your options first, ensure there will be a job waiting at the other end, and truly know what your financial situation will be like at the end of the line. Then decide.

Layby and Hire Purchase

Layby is used when you want to purchase something but you don't have all the money at that time. Kind of like a credit card. But unlike a credit card, which allows you to take home the item but leaves you in debt, layby allows you to pay off the product a little at a time. But you don't get to take the item home until you've paid off the whole amount.

While layby is great if you're not good at saving for things before purchasing, it has the disadvantage that you forget what you've put away and end up spending a lot more for those Christmas presents than you would if you bought everything simultaneously.

Not only that, but if you're buying in advance for children, what are the odds that they've changed their mind on what toys are the greatest and the things they enjoy by the time Christmas rolls around? I know several people who have ended up re-buying gifts because of this.

The other disadvantage to layby is that because you don't have a large figure clogging up your credit card statement, you don't 'see' the amount of debt you actually have. You may have $300 a month leaving your account for various laybys, and while you have the flexibility to pay them off slowly, with no interest accruing, that's still a lot of money walking out the door - usually for items you don't really need.

Hire purchase, unlike layby, lets you use the product while paying it off. Essentially you're hiring an item, only you own it at the end. It is mostly used by businesses for big items like cars and machinery. So what's the difference between hire purchase and a finance lease?

Here's a great comparison[14], but essentially there is one main difference. With a finance lease you don't own anything at the end, and while you usually have the option to purchase, you would have to pay extra for the privilege. With hire purchase you own the item at the end of the term - no extra paid. Essentially it's a payment plan like layby, but with instant access to the item.

So what's the down side? Interest. There has to be something in it for the companies offering hire purchase. They don't get an extra payment at the end of the line but they make plenty along the way with your interest payments. So in reality, hire purchase is no different from personal loans or credit cards. The interest always gets you in the end!

Essentially, whether you decide to put something on layby, on your credit card, or set up a hire purchase there are 3 questions you need to ask yourself first.

1. Do you really need it?
2. Could you get it cheaper somewhere else?

[14] http://aussiecarloans.com.au/blog/lease-vs-hire-purchase/

3. Could you put off buying the item, save the money you need, and buy it outright to avoid interest payments and over-spending?

Thinking about these questions and actually answering them truthfully are two different things. Do yourself a favour and be honest with yourself, and remember: it is better to start at the bottom and climb to the top, than start at the top and sink under the weight of your debt.

Personal Loans and Finance

What about personal loans and finance? Life is comprised of choices. Some people have more choices than others because of upbringing, environment, and other factors, but we all have choices. And whether you truly need a personal loan for a purchase is a choice that people of every walk of life need to make.

Do you need a new car? Yes. Does it need to be straight off the showroom floor? Probably not. I recently did a blog post[15] on my car Viktor. In it, I show how buying an old, second-hand car saved me $74,210 on my mortgage. And no, that isn't a typo. My car truly saved me over 74 grand. But you don't even need to buy an old car. Just not brand spanking new!

Even if you use finance to purchase something, the less you spend, the faster you can pay it off. This means less interest payments so even less in the long run. Don't forget that the cost of the car is not the only cost. Even a good finance deal will still see you paying accumulated interest on top of your car price. Very rarely you'll stumble across a true 0% finance deal, but they are uncommon and usually require you to have a large down payment instead, which people struggle to save.

And then there's the undeniable fact that the money you're forking out to pay for your loan means there's less money to combat other

[15] http://www.how2without.com/meet-viktor/

debt such as student loans and credit cards, which means the interest on that is *also* accruing. Talk about a knock-on effect!

Furniture, kitchens, bathrooms, and bedroom suites. These are all things people use interest free finance deals for, and are all things that you probably don't need. Jump on eBay, Craigslist, Gumtree, or Trade-me and look for a pre-loved item of furniture. Remember we talked previously about not always starting at the top? This is what I mean.

I am writing this now on a $1 table we picked up off eBay, and sitting in chairs that were given to us free by friends. (Thanks Matt and Nic!) They are perfectly serviceable, and while they may not be what I want long-term, they do the job and they cost me next to nothing. Literally!

We paid $84 for a King sofa (the bees knees in Australia) on eBay which had some stains and tears. We covered it with blankets from IKEA, and then 5 years later when I had time and a bit more money I bought fabric and re-covered it. It looks brand new but without the $5,000 price tag. I did receive death by a thousand pinpricks in the process…

My bathroom was new in 1963 and hasn't been touched since then, other than a good scrub and a new toilet seat. And you know what? I can still shower, use the toilet, and even bath half of me at a time. Seriously, I'm only 5 foot 3 (160 cm) and I barely fit in my pygmy bath. How small were people in 1963?

My point is that you don't have to have new things to enjoy life! In fact, when you live with old things for a while, buying something new and pretty, rather than just serviceable, becomes a huge treat, and something you really appreciate.

So think. Do you really need that personal loan? Are you discontent because you truly don't have something serviceable, or simply because it's not up to your high standards? In my first book, *Mortgage*

Free, I discussed feeling 'less' because my house, clothes, car, etc., were so far behind my friends. And the realisation that I came to was that no one cares!

Sure, they might think, "Wow, her bathroom is really rubbish." But that's the end of it. They don't go around for the rest of the year talking about how crappy it is, because the reality is, they've got their own things to think about. And most of the things they're thinking about are far more important to them than your crappy bathroom!

So really, the only thing stopping you from starting with things you can actually afford is your own pride and expectations. If your expectations are that you must have everything new and top of the line from day one, then that's fine. But you'll also need to understand that those expectations come with a heavy burden of debt that will take years to recover from.

Is it worth it?

Direct Debits and Subscriptions

Something that's almost worse (almost) than credit card debt are monthly subscriptions. Why? Because unlike a credit card bill that you see every month, they are set and forget. You set up a payment and then whether you use the service or not you continue to pay them. Month after month and year after year.

You can even set up a monthly subscription on your credit card now, something you never used to be able to do, which gives you the double whammy of a monthly expense AND credit card debt!

Your challenge for this chapter is to go through your bank account and find all your direct debits, and really question if you actually need them. Don't just go through and say, "Cable, yup, I really need that. Spotify, yup, I use that all the time. Meal planning, that makes my life so much simpler."

I want you to get a pen and write down everything that is coming out of your bank account on a regular basis that is not necessary to your survival (rent, food, clothes, insurance, etc.). Then add it all up for the month. Multiply it by 12 and then really ask yourself, "Do I want to be spending this much money every year on these things?" As with the finance snapshot, there is a free graph on my website[16] to help you with this.

Am I using that gym membership? Could I get by with the free version of Spotify? Do I watch all the cable channels covered in my plan? My friend's mum in the UK recently looked over her cable and phone plan, realised she only watched a fraction of the channels, and downgraded. She still has the channels she actually uses, her phone, and Internet, and she's only paying 80 pounds a month now instead of £150! That's a massive saving of 840 pounds a year!

Recap:

- Credit card debt is sitting at $15,000 per person, and for many it is much higher
- Interest on debt means you end up paying much more off in the long run
- Cutting back on small things can save you thousands of dollars a year
- Start from the bottom and work your way to the top

So if you're wondering how you can afford to pay off debt or start saving for something you truly want, start by looking at what you're already spending. Where can you cut back? What can you do to curb your spending? Anyway, more on that up next in *Chapter 6 - Getting*

[16] http://www.how2without.com/the-real-cost-of-direct-debits/

Rid of Debt, the Worst Houseguest Ever. For now, work out what those direct debits are really costing you!

CHAPTER 6:
GETTING RID OF DEBT, THE WORST HOUSEGUEST EVER

There are a few solutions for dealing with debt. You need to pick the one that suits you the most. Read through them all, sit down with your partner in crime, and look at where your debt is now, where you want to be in the future, and the best route possible for making that happen.

1. **Pay it off**

Pour all your money into your debt, starting with the one with the highest interest rate, and GET RID OF IT!

This is what I think of as the best option.

You can use the budgets within this book to knock off debt, instead of saving, or paying off a mortgage. The process is the same for all 3.

Choose a budget that focuses on saving money each month. This doesn't have to be as rigid as a certain percentage of your pay. You may decide to use the boot camp budget and cut things out each week to save money. Whatever works for you is fine. Then take those savings and use them to start paying chunks of money off your debt.

Do short blasts of debt payments and then have a break. For example, put every bit of leftover money you can lay your hands on into your debt for three weeks of the month. Then for the last week, relax and spend some of it.

This means you really smash your debt, without giving up because you miss your money! If you've been through the budgeting portion of the book, you've probably got a good idea of what's going to work for you, and your level of debt will decide what route you take.

The lower your debt, the more you should focus on getting rid of it - it will only get bigger with interest payments added, and neither of the other options really apply for small debts.

Once your debt is gone you can focus on saving money for things that you really want and are a lot more exciting than getting rid of debt!

2. **Consolidate your debt**

If you know that your debt will never get paid off unless it is direct debited out of your bank account, or you get flustered trying to deal with multiple bills each month, then look at consolidation.

Google 'debt consolidation' and you will get hit with a stack of companies eager to help you out. Why? The interest they stand to earn on your loan. They might be saving you money, but don't kid yourself, they are in it for a reason too, and it isn't the good karma.

Debt consolidation is great for people who have a lot of different types and amounts of debts rather than just a few small ones to pay off.

It basically works by grouping all your debts into one, making them easier to manage. Usually, you can also obtain a lower interest rate than what you're paying.

Obviously, the length of the loans and the interest rates below are indicative only, they vary vastly from country to country and person to person, but here's an example for you:

You have 8 different forms of debt. The flat screen TV and the lounge suite were both purchased with an interest-free finance deal that is due to run out. The other loans are all accruing interest already.

Type of loan	Cost	Interest	Length of loan
Car loan	$18,000	6%	10 years
Lounge suite	$3,800	14%	2 years after interest free
Credit card	$2,500	12%	Unlimited time
Credit card	$10,000	18%	Unlimited time
Credit card	$1,200	16%	Unlimited time
Student loan	$18,000	7%	Unlimited time
Personal loan-holiday	$10,000	15%	5 years
Flat screen TV	$4,000	14%	2 years after interest-free
	$67,500 TOTAL		

These give you a total of $67,500 in debt. Holy crap! You owe $67,500!! Just kidding. (-:

Seriously though - that's bad and you need to get rid of it. If you scraped together $740 per week to pay off your debts (remember this is a big debt amount - it wouldn't be this high for most people) and set yourself a 2-year time frame to be debt free, this is what your minimum repayments and interest amounts would look like.

Type of loan	Loan amount	Time at minimum payment	Total paid
Credit card #1 18% Interest	$10,000	$117- minimum payment- 2 years	$12,165
Credit card #2 16% Interest	$1,200	$16- minimum payment- 2 years	$1,644
Personal loan 15% Interest	$10,000	$114- minimum payment- 2 years	$11,829
Lounge Suite 14% Interest	$3,800	$44- minimum payment- 2 years	$4,602
Flat screen TV 14% Interest	$4,000	$46- minimum payment- 2 years	$4,831
Credit card #3 12% Interest	$2500	$29- minimum payment- 2 years	$3,055
Student Loan 7% Interest	$18,000	$188- minimum payment- 2 years	$19,541
Car loan 6% Interest	$18,000	$186- minimum payment- 2 years	$19,352
TOTALS	**$67,500- TOTAL DEBT**	**$740 per week- MINIMUM PAYMENT 2 YEARS**	**$77,019- TOTAL PAID IN 2 YEARS**

So over 2 years you have paid an extra $10,000 in interest. This isn't as bad as it could be though. Spread these same debts out over a 10-year period and you would pay $120,693. Almost twice your original debt. Bottom line is: interest payments on debt are lethal!

Let's imagine you choose a debt consolidation company called Debt-Rid (purely fictional) to help you consolidate your loans. They are offering interest rates of 10% for the life of your loan.

Your student loan and car loan both have lower interest rates, but the three credit cards, personal loan, and the TV and furniture loans are all higher. Debt-Rid sets up a loan of $31,500 and you pay off all your loans. Woo-hoo!

Except now you owe Debt-Rid $31,500. How is this any better?

Simply put, you will be paying less interest (if you did your research and picked a good one), and as your debts are all in one place they are much easier to keep track of and pay.

You are now left with only 3 monthly bills. As you can see the total is the same—you haven't actually paid any of your debt off, just consolidated it into fewer loans.

Type of Loan	Cost	Interest	Length of Loan
Car loan	$18,000	6%	10 years
Student loan	$18,000	7%	Unlimited time
Debt-rid loan	$31,500	10%	2 years
	$67,500		

Now your debt is consolidated, pay the minimum amount required on the car and student loans, and pour all your extra cash into paying off the Debt Rid loan, as this has the highest interest and will cost you the most in the long run. Once this is gone, tackle the student loan and then the car loan.

Always check to make sure there are no fees attached to your loans for paying them off fast. You don't want to do all that work only to be hit with massive fees! Make sure you choose a debt consolidation service that either doesn't have early repayment fees, or would be happy to waive them. Remember, they *want* your business - they stand to earn a lot of money from the interest you pay on your loan.

Type of Loan	Weekly amount 1 1 year 2 months	Weekly amount 2 5 months	Weekly amount 3 4 months	Total paid
Debt-rid 10% Interest	$578 (maximum you can afford)	-PAID-	-PAID-	$33,131
Student loan 7% Interest	$82 (minimum payment)	$660 ($578+$82)	-PAID-	$19,375
Car loan 6% interest	$80 minimum payment	Maintain $80	$740 ($578+$82 +$80)	$19,580
	$740 total each week	**$740 total each week**	**$740 total each week**	**$72,086**

This is a rough estimate of how your repayments would look. Total paid over all debts was $72,086 and it took under 2 years to get yourself debt free. This is based on a large debt, however. Not all debts will take this long or cost this much to be free of.

If you could only afford to pay off half that amount every week, you could still be debt free in 5 years. Now that's not impossible, is it? Notice that the total amount paid is $5,000 less with debt consolidation than without?

3. Add to your debts

If your debts are too large and will take years to pay off even when throwing everything at them, and you really want to buy a house, or already have a home, then look at adding to your debt with a home loan, or re-drawing your current one. I know, I know, WTF, right!?

Why is this craziness an option?

Houses usually increase in value over the years, and you may find yourself sitting on a home with great equity, without having paid off a cent. Our home is worth twice today what we paid for it 8 years ago - through no work of our own. If this happens, then a seemingly stupid move can become an awesome one.

And… because some people are just rubbish at paying off debt. My husband was friends with a man whose wife loved to spend. They had a home, but they could never renovate or upgrade because his wage every month went to paying off the latest credit card bill. So, he redrew on his mortgage, put in a pool, renovated his property and had to pay more on his mortgage every month.

His wife could no longer spend money because they simply didn't have it. They were maxed out paying their increased mortgage. Now, while I wouldn't suggest running off to do the same, I can totally understand where he was coming from. He felt it was better to have something to show for the money that was being spent every week, than for it to just keep being frittered away.

If this is you, then look at doing the same. Often the interest payable on mortgages is much less than those on credit cards and personal loans. Could you re-draw, pay all your bills, and then settle into a larger weekly mortgage payment? Have a chat with your accountant or a financial adviser and go through the figures with them.

There is a catch though. If you do this, you CANNOT keep spending the way you were. The whole idea is to get you back to a base point so you can start fresh, not so you can start building up your debt again.

The debt you had is still there, it has just been reshuffled so that it forces you to pay it each week, rather than building up. Cut up your credit cards, take out cash every week for your spending money, use every tip we talk about in *Chapter 15* if you have to, but stop spending!

Recap:

- Paying debt off early is the best option.
- Paying debt off fast will save you big money on interest payments in the long run.
- Debt consolidation is great for people who have a lot of different types of debt.
- Work on spending less so you can pay off more.

Debt is a hard thing to get rid of, but once it's gone, you will be in a much better situation financially, and the world seems to open itself up to you. Things that seemed impossible before are now seen as achievable, and life takes on a whole different viewpoint.

If you are having trouble getting your head around your bills, interest rates, and finances, book yourself in with a financial planner and let them do the legwork. The few hundred you pay them will be worth it to sort yourself out and put a plan into action.

Next up: find out why budgeting, paying off debt, and goals should always be used together, in *Chapter 7 - Budgeting and Goals: Same-same but Different.*

CHAPTER 7:
BUDGETING AND GOALS. SAME-SAME BUT DIFFERENT

The budgets that work well, and are easier to stick to, are those that have goals attached. All budgets have goals, but some are tenuous at best. Finding out what I spend my money on may well be a goal, but it's not exactly one that fills me with excitement and anticipation! I'm talking about the stuff you dream about. Those things that you fall asleep thinking of, and spend your day fantasizing over.

This might be a holiday to a tropical island, saving for a house, buying that hair straightener you've always wanted (don't laugh; it's one of my goals), or buying a new car. Your goals don't have to be big, either. You may just want to buy some odds and ends for your home, eat out more frequently, or take your kids somewhere fun for the day. Whatever that thing is that keeps niggling you - make it a goal.

Have debt you need to pay off first? Still make goals! Make your final goal zero debt, but set yourself smaller goals on the way there. If you have a large amount of debt that will take a couple of years to pay off, you're going to need some joy along the way. Do I need to say it again? Make goals.

Goals are a powerful tool when budgeting. When you decide on something that you want, and set up a plan on how to achieve that goal, it suddenly becomes more possible than it ever has before. Because your goal seems more possible, you are less likely to give up and much more likely to persevere, and ultimately, succeed.

Some budgets are more goal oriented than others. Your budget doesn't have to be a bucket list of things to do, although it can be if that suits you. Some people may find they only need one large goal to motivate themselves. Others may find that a series of smaller goals work better. We will go over how to find a budget in *Chapter 13: What's Your Type? Which Budget Suits You Best?* For now, though, I've got some homework for you.

Grab yourself a piece of paper and a pen, and write down everything that you daydream about. I've given you some examples below, but make sure you really focus on the things that are important to *you.* Another fun way of doing this is to make a picture collage of your goals. This is a much more visual approach, and you can hang it in your room once you're done, as a daily reminder.

To do this, just cut pictures from magazines, travel brochures, or any other medium. You could also print pictures to use. Glue them all onto a big sheet of paper or card, along with any quotes or sayings you think might give it some pizzazz. I have one of these picture boards hung up at the moment for the outside of my house.

We desperately need to re-clad our home as the old fibro is letting all the damp in, and you know, asbestos is bad! So my current goal is to get this done. It's a pretty boring goal, I know, but my picture board has exterior house and garden designs, wooden decks, lighting, and windows. Every time I look at it I envisage how our home will look once it's done, and it encourages me to persevere. It's not going to be cheap, so this is my final goal; I have a few smaller ones to keep me going along the way.

Here's a list of examples over a few areas, to help jog your memory and write your goals list. Aim for a list of at least 10 goals and then place them in order of importance to you. You can add notes to yourself too, like, 'wanted this for ages,' 'will cost about $5,000,' or 'wouldn't take long to reach this.' Write, glue, and dream, until you have a list or board that makes you excited just looking at it!

Budgeting and Goals	
Adventures	**Physical**
Hang-gliding	Coffee machine
Overseas holidays	New Car
Day trip to the aquarium	Bigger TV
Visit a neighbouring town	Beautiful shoes
Investing	**Financial Future**
Buy a house	Retirement fund
Invest in stocks	Becoming debt free
Education	Emergency money
Buy a rental property	Starting a business

I find it helpful to have short-term and long-term goals. As I mentioned, my long-term goal is to get the house re-clad. I also have short-term goals such as visiting family in New Zealand more often, going on family camping trips, and doing some 'girls' weekends' away.

Sometimes even a picture board is not enough to continue motivating you when your big goal seems so far away. Having small goals along the way really helps boost your sense of accomplishment, and encourages you to stick at it.

You should now have a list of at least 10 items that make you super excited and raring to start budgeting. If you're not excited, then these are not the goals you want, but rather the goals you think you should have. Let me tell you now, they won't work. Not unless you have the willpower of a machine. And even if you do achieve them, you won't have much enthusiasm for continuing on to your next goal. Because you've already used up all that willpower.

I get it, believe me. Do you think I truly believe cladding the house is exciting? No. But the thought of how great the house will look, how much less cleaning there will be without the damp, having a massive deck that will become an entertainment space - now those are exciting! So even if you set yourself a goal that is more need than want, make sure you look for the joy in it. And get excited!

Recap:

- The budgets that work are those with goals attached.
- Goals are a powerful tool as they motivate and inspire.
- Catalogue your goals by creating a list or a picture board.
- Create short-term and long-term goals.
- Look for the joy in your goals and get excited!

Print off[17] the fillable examples list and start dreaming! Now take a look at the tried and true budgets that have been helping people hang onto their money for generations in *Chapter 8: Traditional Budgets. Old Tricks, New Dogs*. Are you excited yet?

[17] http://www.how2without.com/bonus-materials/bbdd-pdf-workbook/

CHAPTER 8:
TRADITIONAL BUDGETS: OLD TRICKS, NEW DOGS

Traditional budgets are the ones that spring to mind when you hear the term budgeting. It's the paper graph or spreadsheet, or even a simple row of figures in a ledger. They are tried and tested methods that have been used, tweaked, and used again, with much success.

If you are someone who enjoys figures, the simple pleasure of adding and subtracting, and likes to 'see' where your money is going, then odds are you will really enjoy these budgets.

Budget 1: Spreadsheet/Line item

The original budget, and one of the most successful, is the spreadsheet budget. Spreadsheet budgets require little knowledge or ability, and are readily accessible on the Internet. They are also the budget that most people give up on, because they offer nothing except figures.

Here's how the process works:

To create a spreadsheet budget, you itemise every area of your spending. Not just categories, but specific items such as groceries, bills, petrol, etc., and specify a dollar amount for each. You work backwards from your income amount until all your income is used, and each item has an amount that can be spent on it.

1. Complete the 10 step budgeting process in *Chapter 3*.
2. Download a fillable spreadsheet graph[18] or make your own.

---

[18] http://www.how2without.com/bonus-materials/bbdd-pdf-workbook/

3. Starting with your income at the top, start subtracting off expenses with known costs such as rent/mortgage, recurring bills, and subscriptions.

4. Then minus off expenses with an estimated amount such as groceries, infrequent bills, petrol, and work/school expenses.

5. Take note of what is left (if any) and allocate this to savings and spending.

6. If you find your income does not cover all your known and estimated expenses, you need to either look at other ways of making money, or minimise your spending (this is usually the better option). Go back through your budget and look at everything that could be cut or minimized to create a more streamlined and efficient budget and then try again.

   Be realistic! One of the biggest reasons a budget fails is that people try to cut back in areas that just don't work.

7. Use your budget for a few weeks and then review it once you know what is working and what is not. Don't be afraid to make changes where necessary.

SPREADSHEET BUDGET

House Expenses	Projected Cost	Actual Cost	Difference
Mortgage or Rent			
Electricity			
Water			
Sewage			
Phone			
Gas			
Rates			
Maintainence and Repairs			
Total			

Transportation	Projected Cost	Actual Cost	Difference
Car lease/ payments			
Bus/ taxi/ train fare			
Fuel			
Insurance			
Licencing			
Registration			
Maintainence and Repairs			
Parking fees			
Total			

Insurance and Fees	Projected Cost	Actual Cost	Difference
Home Insurance			
Health Insurance			
Life Insurance			
School fees			
Travel Insurance			
Business Insurance			
Pet Insurance			
Total			

Living Expenses	Projected Cost	Actual Cost	Difference
Groceries			
Eating out			
Total			

SPREADSHEET BUDGET

Health and Personal Care	Projected Cost	Actual Cost	Difference
Medical			
Hair/ Nails			
Clothing			
Gym/ Health club Membership			
Dry cleaning			
Vet expenses			
Total			

Extras	Projected Cost	Actual Cost	Difference
Spending money			
Travel/ Holidays			
Donations			
Gifts			
Unexpected Bills			
Total			

Entertainment	Projected Cost	Actual Cost	Difference
Movies/ DVD			
Coffee/ Meals out			
Live shows/ Concerts			
Sporting Events			
Days Out			
Netflix subscription			
Spotify/ iTunes subscription			
Total			

Savings and Investment	Projected Cost	Actual Cost	Difference
Super/ Retirement savings			
Savings Money			
Investment Portfolio			
Total			

SPREADSHEET BUDGET

Debt/ Loans	Projected Cost	Actual Cost	Difference
Car loan			
Mortgage payment			
Student loan			
Credit Card payments			
Layby/ Hire purchase/ Finance			
Personal Loan			
Total			

Totals	Projected Total	Actual Total	Difference
House Insurance			
Transportation			
Insurance and Fees			
Living Expenses			
Health and Personal Care			
Extra			
Entertainment			
Savings and Investments			
Debt/ Loans			

Income	Projected Income	Actual Income	Difference
Job 1			
Job 2			
Interest			
Investment Income			
Gifts			
Passive Income			

Totals vs Income	Projected	Actual	Difference
Total Expenses			
Total Income			
Plus/ Minus			

Pros:

- Because you are allocating spending to specific items rather than categories, you have a very firm grasp on what you spend your money on every week.
- Spreadsheets can be as simple or as complex as you want to make them
- It is easy to adjust your budget if you can see an area is not performing as you expected it to.
- Once set up, spreadsheet budgets are easy to maintain.

Cons:

- Spreadsheet budgets can be quite time heavy, as you need to look at all your spending - cash and card - to set them up. You also have to spend time every week adding up your expenditures and making sure they fit within your budget parameters.
- They're boring. There are no goals attached to get excited about and no bright colours or pie charts (unless you do an online version).
- You need to be able to add and subtract with ease.
- You can feel very restricted as every cent of your money is accounted for.

Tips and Tricks:

You can set up separate accounts to store your savings and bill money in. This way, they roll over each week until needed, without being frittered away. Always make sure you allocate enough spending money, as you will end up with a deficit in other areas if you budget with what you would *like* to spend, rather than what you *actually* spend.

Attributes for Spreadsheet Budget

1- BUDGET TYPE			
My budget should have	Pictures & Graphs	Figures & Facts	Both
My budget should be	Colour	Black and White	Both
This budget is for	Just me	My family	Other
I like budgets that are	Traditional	Non-traditional	New
I want a budget that's	Simple	Neutral	Complex
I want my budget to focus on	Goals	Savings	Making ends meet
I want a budget that is	Flexible	Itemized	Categorized

2- TIME AND COST			
Time a week I can spend on my budget	10 minutes	Under an hour	Under two hours
I want a one off setup time	As short as possible	Under an hour	Anything
I want a budget that costs	Nothing	One-time fee	Ongoing cost

3- KNOWLEDGE			
My math level/tolerance	I hate math	I don't mind math	I'm a math guru
I understand how to use a budget	Not at all	Basic knowledge	In-depth knowledge
I want to know where my money goes	Not at all	Neutral	Definitely
I want to budget	Not at all	Somewhat	Definitely

4- FUTURE PLANNING			
I am saving for	Retirement	Investing	Goals
I want a budget for	Short term	Long term	Don't know
I have these types of debt	Car loan	Student loan	Other debt
I have these types of debt	Credit card	Layby/hire purchase	Personal loan

5- TECHNOLOGY			
Technology and I are	Enemies	Acquaintances	Friends
I want to do my budget	On paper	On the computer	On my phone
I want to sync my budget to	Other tech items	Social media	Nothing!

6- SPENDING HABITS			
When I spend money I use	Mostly cash	Mostly card	Both
When I spend money it's	Spontaneous	Planned	Both
When I see something I really want I	Can walk away	Have to buy it	Different each day
At the end of the week I	Have money left	Am always broke	Different each week

Budget 2: Category/ Envelope

Instead of assigning a dollar amount to specific items like the spreadsheet budget, the envelope budget assigns an amount to specific categories. So instead of water, power, and rates each having a spend amount, you would just have a 'bills' category. I love the simplicity of envelope budgeting, and I know many people who it has worked really well for. It's easy to set up, and you have a firm grasp on how much you're spending in each area.

Here's how the process works:

The category budget can be done in a very tactile way or simply a visual way. If you like a more hands-on approach, then you can sort your money into envelopes. Actual envelopes with cash money, one envelope for each category: Bills, Household expenses, Spending, etc. This is a very tangible way of categorizing your spending and helps you see how each spend diminishes your total. No money - no spending.

If you prefer not to have envelopes of cash lying around, then you can do the exact same thing online. Just set up several bank accounts and label them with your category names. Each time you get paid, separate your money into the categories straight away, and then use them as needed. Categories such as bills may build up over a period of time and then be depleted in one week as bills come in. Other accounts such as household expenses may be a lot more fluid, and will need a debit card assigned to them.

The best way to use this budget is to not have a credit card, for the simple fact that it is both hard to keep track of, and easy to spend money you don't have. If you do choose to have one, make sure you sort your card expenses out according to category each month, and pay it off with the money you put aside for each.

1. Complete the 10 step budgeting process in *Chapter 3*.

2. Decide on how much each category will need. If you get stuck download this form[19] to help you.

3. Get envelopes and stuff them with cash OR create bank accounts to separate your income into.

4. Spend only the money you have in your envelope/account for each category

5. Save any remaining money, or use it to get out of debt or to invest.

6. Use your budget for a few weeks and then review it once you know what is working and what is not. Don't be afraid to make changes where necessary.

[19] http://www.how2without.com/bonus-materials/bbdd-pdf-workbook/

CATEGORY BUDGET

House Expenses	Projected Cost	Actual Cost	Difference
Mortgage/ Rent/ Household Bills			

Transportation	Projected Cost	Actual Cost	Difference
Fuel/ Transport/ Insurance			

Insurance and Fees	Projected Cost	Actual Cost	Difference
Home/ Health/ Life Insurance			

Living Expenses	Projected Cost	Actual Cost	Difference
Groceries/ Eating out			

Health and Personal Care	Projected Cost	Actual Cost	Difference
Medical/ Hair/ Gym membership			

Extras	Projected Cost	Actual Cost	Difference
Spending money/ Travel/ Holidays			

Entertainment	Projected Cost	Actual Cost	Difference
Movies/ Shows/ Days out/ Netflix			

Savings and Investment	Projected Cost	Actual Cost	Difference
Super/ Retirement/ Investment			

CATEGORY BUDGET

Debt/ Loans	Projected Cost	Actual Cost	Difference
Car loan/ Credit cards/ Personal loan			

Totals	Projected Total	Actual Total	Difference

Income	Projected Income	Actual Income	Difference
Job/ Investments/ Interest			

Totals vs Income	Projected	Actual	Difference
Total Expenses			
Total Income			
Plus/ Minus			

Pros:

- If you are diligent with sticking to your categories, you can't over-spend. Once the money in a particular envelope is gone - it's gone. Spending simply can't happen.
- It can help you build discipline where spending is involved, and teach you to be more in tune with your money and your budget.
- Although it's not the purpose, your savings can be used as an emergency fund if need be; something that many people just don't have.

- Because you can actively see how much money you have left in your envelope, you tend to think more carefully about each purchase, leading to much more mindfulness when it comes to your money.

- No overdraft or credit card fees. You will always be spending only the cash you have, not borrowing money, so no nasty bank fees.

- No more missed payments. You won't have to wait to get paid to pay a bill, the money will be sitting there waiting, meaning you pay on time, every time.

Cons:

- It can be hard to stick to your categories and not 'steal' money from other envelopes.

- You have to withdraw cash from an ATM (not many of us get paid in cash). And then you have to carry cash around. (If you're doing things the traditional way)

- It's tough to get a whole family using (and recording) cash, when plastic is just so easy.

- It is not as convenient as paying by card.

- You won't get credit card rewards - and some people do really well out of these!

Tips and Tricks:

Buy a wallet that separates your cash into separate sections, with the ability to label each section as you like. These are readily available on crafty sites such as Etsy[20]. Have an envelope within each category,

---

[20] www.etsy.com

with a small amount of 'backup' money set aside. It's easy to burn through all your category money without realising it. The backup money is great for tiding you over till you get paid again, without breaking into your other envelopes.

Load money onto fuel or transport cards so you never have the excuse of taking a credit card with you for 'emergencies.' Instead of having a credit card for emergencies, take a debit card, which has a finite amount of cash on it - but still only use it for emergencies.

Attributes for Category Budget

1- BUDGET TYPE			
My budget should have	Pictures & Graphs	Figures & Facts	Both
My budget should be	Colour	Black and White	Both
This budget is for	Just me	My family	Other
I like budgets that are	Traditional	Non-traditional	New
I want a budget that's	Simple	Neutral	Complex
I want my budget to focus on	Goals	Savings	Making ends meet
I want a budget that is	Flexible	Itemized	Categorized

2- TIME AND COST			
Time a week I can spend on my budget	10 minutes	Under an hour	Under two hours
I want a one off setup time	As short as possible	Under an hour	Anything
I want a budget that costs	Nothing	One-time fee	Ongoing cost

3- KNOWLEDGE			
My math level/tolerance	I hate math	I don't mind math	I'm a math guru
I understand how to use a budget	Not at all	Basic knowledge	In-depth knowledge
I want to know where my money goes	Not at all	Neutral	Definitely
I want to budget	Not at all	Somewhat	Definitely

4- FUTURE PLANNING			
I am saving for	Retirement	Investing	Goals
I want a budget for	Short term	Long term	Don't know
I have these types of debt	Car loan	Student loan	Other debt
I have these types of debt	Credit card	Layby/hire purchase	Personal loan

5- TECHNOLOGY			
Technology and I are	Enemies	Acquaintances	Friends
I want to do my budget	On paper	On the computer	On my phone
I want to sync my budget to	Other tech items	Social media	Nothing!

6- SPENDING HABITS			
When I spend money I use	Mostly cash	Mostly card	Both
When I spend money it's	Spontaneous	Planned	Both
When I see something I really want I	Can walk away	Have to buy it	Different each day
At the end of the week I	Have money left	Am always broke	Different each week

Recap:

- Spreadsheet budget: Uses your income as a base and then works backwards to zero, attaching a dollar amount to all your expenses, savings, and spending money. Also called the zero sum budget.
- Category/Envelope budget: Splits your income into separate categories or envelopes, for things such as bills, spending, household expenses and saving. Doesn't itemize individual things.

Like what you've seen? Download the worksheets[21] to help you get started. If traditional budgets aren't your cup of tea, then take a gander at the next ones we've gathered up in *Chapter 9: Non-Traditional Budgets: Fresh Ideas for Modern Lives*. You'll still end up achieving the same goals, you'll just take a different route getting there.

---

[21] http://www.how2without.com/bonus-materials/bbdd-pdf-workbook/

CHAPTER 9:

NON-TRADITIONAL BUDGETS: FRESH IDEAS FOR MODERN LIVES

So, you want a budget, but the thought of doing a spreadsheet makes you cringe. I know exactly how you feel… There is much more to budgeting than columns and math, however, and I've collected my favourites for you to have a gander at. They still help you manage your money, but in lots of alternate ways. Enjoy!

Budget 1: Bucket list

The bucket list budget is goal oriented. It doesn't focus on any other area except your next goal. Don't get me wrong, you've still got to figure out what you're spending where, and how you can cut back to build your savings, but once that's done you only focus on the savings each week. That means no endless numbers, or budget rehashing. In fact, you never even have to think about it.

I tend to approach this budget like a ladder. I don't just have one goal in mind, but a list of them. You can even draw yourself a ladder and have each rung as a goal. Visualize yourself climbing that ladder, and each goal reached is another rung higher.

Here's how the process works:

Say I want to go on a 2-month rock climbing trip around Asia. I know I'm going to need around $5,000, so this is one of my goals. I'm going to need a level of fitness greater than I have now. I make another goal to be able to run 5 kms easily. Note to self - buy new shoes. Another goal is to climb grade 24's (rock-climbing levels). Another goal is to book and pay for flights and accommodation. And I need to find someone to mind my house and pets while I'm gone.

As you can see, while they are separate goals, they all complement one another. You don't get so overwhelmed as when they are all grouped together, and you get an awesome sense of accomplishment when you reach each goal. You can put a time limit on each goal too, which helps to motivate you, or you can just reach them in your own time.

The goals don't have to be linked, though. You may just like to have a list of separate goals, such as: Buy a new TV, visit a new country, buy a first edition of your favourite book, and spend a weekend shopping at the mall. Whatever your goals - make them fun, make them many, and make some easy to reach, and some harder.

1. Complete the 10-step budgeting process in *Chapter 3.*

2. Work out how much money you have 'free' at the end of each week.

3. Set a goal, or several goals you want to achieve, either as one final goal or in a ladder format with a series of goals. See our fillable form[22] for an easy starting point.

4. Make a time line (or print ours[23]), which takes into account how much 'free money' you have, and the cost of the goals you have chosen.

5. Use visual artwork or scrapbooking to encourage yourself and remind you of your goals. Hang your timeline somewhere, or write it into your diary so you can keep track of your progress.

---

[22] http://www.how2without.com/bonus-materials/bbdd-pdf-workbook/

[23] http://www.how2without.com/bonus-materials/bbdd-pdf-workbook/

6. Set aside your goal money every week. No excuses.
7. Set a new goal each time one is reached. This will keep you moving forward and constantly achieving your dreams.

GOAL PLANNER

Goal:
Cost:
Completed bv:

Goal:
Cost:
Completed bv:

Goal:
Cost:
Completed bv:

Goal:
Cost:
Completed bv:

Goal:
Cost:
Completed bv:

Goal:
Cost:
Completed bv:

Goal:
Cost:
Completed bv:

Pros:

- Goals are a powerful tool when budgeting. Using short- and long-term goals boosts your sense of accomplishment and encourages you to achieve your dreams.

- Splitting your goal into several steps makes this budget more manageable and fun than most, as it seems like you are constantly succeeding. Because you are!

- Goal-based budgets don't need you to forever be looking at your spending. They focus only on the saving and goal aspect.

Cons:

- Because of its focus on only the savings portion of your budget, you don't really have any idea of what you are spending on everything else.

- Many people use bucket list budgets to achieve only fun goals, such as travel and trivial buys. Things like saving for a house or investing are never budgeted for. Or they go the other way, only creating hard-to-achieve goals, and losing interest fast because of it. Balance, Daniel-san! (Overused, I know…)

- It can be easy to pilfer your goal money to use for 'emergencies,' as there is a lump sum sitting there. As you are not focused on your spending with this budget, excess still occurs, and it is simpler for most people to take their goal money than to cut back their spending.

Tips and Tricks:

The best way to achieve your bucket list goals is to set up a direct debit with your savings amount each week to a different bank. This means you won't be tempted to touch it. If you can't see it, it won't call to you! Even better, don't set up your savings account with a debit card or Internet banking. This means you have to physically front up to the bank to get your money out.

Tell people about your goals, or encourage some friends to complete them with you. If you want to do a shark dive, find someone who wants to do one too, and help each other stay on target.

Attributes for Bucket List Budget

1- BUDGET TYPE			
My budget should have	Pictures & Graphs	Figures & Facts	Both
My budget should be	Colour	Black and White	Both
This budget is for	Just me	My family	Other
I like budgets that are	Traditional	Non-traditional	New
I want a budget that's	Simple	Neutral	Complex
I want my budget to focus on	Goals	Savings	Making ends meet
I want a budget that is	Flexible	Itemized	Categorized

2- TIME AND COST			
Time a week I can spend on my budget	10 minutes	Under an hour	Under two hours
I want a one off setup time	As short as possible	Under an hour	Anything
I want a budget that costs	Nothing	One-time fee	Ongoing cost

3- KNOWLEDGE			
My math level/tolerance	I hate math	I don't mind math	I'm a math guru
I understand how to use a budget	Not at all	Basic knowledge	In-depth knowledge
I want to know where my money goes	Not at all	Neutral	Definitely
I want to budget	Not at all	Somewhat	Definitely

4- FUTURE PLANNING			
I am saving for	Retirement	Investing	Goals
I want a budget for	Short term	Long term	Don't know
I have these types of debt	Car loan	Student loan	Other debt
I have these types of debt	Credit card	Layby/hire purchase	Personal loan

5- TECHNOLOGY			
Technology and I are	Enemies	Acquaintances	Friends
I want to do my budget	On paper	On the computer	On my phone
I want to sync my budget to	Other tech items	Social media	Nothing!

6- SPENDING HABITS			
When I spend money I use	Mostly cash	Mostly card	Both
When I spend money it's	Spontaneous	Planned	Both
When I see something I really want I	Can walk away	Have to buy it	Different each day
At the end of the week I	Have money left	Am always broke	Different each week

Budget 2: Cashless

Do you spend money on random things if your wallet is full? Then the cashless budget could be for you. It's based on a very simple premise - never take any money with you. You can take a card with you for large expenses such as petrol and groceries, but it limits all the little expenditure that fritters your money away every week.

You have to be pretty strong-willed for this to work, as with the ability to use your debit or credit card for even small amounts now, you could end up spending just as much.

Here's how the process works:

The name kind of gives it away. With the cashless budget, you eliminate all forms of cash spending, and only spend on credit and debit cards what you need to. You can load a debit card with your weekly spend amount and use this for all your expenses. You still need to be mindful of what you spend, but you can easily keep track of your money by looking at your bank's transaction listings.

Often with cash you just don't know what you have spent your money on. A cashless system helps you create a greater understanding of your spending habits, and what you can do to improve them. You don't even have to complete the 10-step budgeting process if you don't want to. Just continue on as you normally do, but use your card for everything. You can then review and revise once you've created a spending snapshot. You'd be surprised what you spend your money on!

1. If you don't have any idea what you're spending, complete the 10-step process in *Chapter 3*. Otherwise just start at step 2.

2. Draw up or print[24] a cashless budget form like the one below, and fill it out.

3. Get rid of all the cash in your house. Bank it - don't spend it!

4. Set up direct debits where you can, for recurring bills and subscriptions. Minimise subscriptions and bills to achieve your future spend goals.

5. If you don't already have one, create a savings account (without a debit card attached) and set up a direct deposit each week of your savings amount (make sure this amount is sustainable long term).

6. Leave your credit cards stashed somewhere at home, and only use them in an emergency.

7. Have one debit card with your remaining money (after savings and direct debits) that you carry with you. Use this for your day-to-day expenses such as food and petrol. Once the money is gone you can't spend any more, so no debt.

8. Review your bank transactions every month, and work out where you are still spending excess money. Try to eliminate this spending where you can, and alter your budget to reflect these changes.

Current spend is how much you are spending in each area now. Future spend is how much you would like to spend or save by using this budget, and Difference is the monetary difference between the two. It shows you how much you will need to save in each area to meet your goals.

---

[24] http://www.how2without.com/bonus-materials/bbdd-pdf-workbook/

CASHLESS BUDGET

	Current spend	Future spend	Difference
Income	$850	$850	$0
Direct Debits, Recurring bills & subscriptions	$325	$250	-$75
Savings	$0	$150	$150
Daily expenses	$525	$450	-$75
Total	$850	$850	$0

Pros:

- You no longer have money in your pocket to spend on random things.
- It is much easier to keep track of what you spend your money on by reviewing your card transactions.
- You don't have to keep cash receipts and enter them into your spending each week
- Budgeting can all be done online, in the comfort of your own home.

Cons:

- You have to have access to online banking to make this work properly.
- You can still use your card almost anywhere for small purchases, which means you can end up spending just as much!

- You don't have coins for things such as parking or school donation days, which are a necessary evil.
- It doesn't give you a firm grasp of budgeting and how to spend less, it just minimizes the spending you do.

Tips and Tricks:

Give yourself a baseline of what you can spend on a card. For example - you can't use your card for any purchase under $50. This means that bills, petrol and groceries are covered, but lunches, coffees, and personal shopping is not. This doesn't mean you can go out and buy a $100 handbag, it just stops the little expenditures that add up every week to large amounts!

Attributes for Cashless Budget

1- BUDGET TYPE			
My budget should have	Pictures & Graphs	Figures & Facts	Both
My budget should be	Colour	Black and White	Both
This budget is for	Just me	My family	Other
I like budgets that are	Traditional	Non-traditional	New
I want a budget that's	Simple	Neutral	Complex
I want my budget to focus on	Goals	Savings	Making ends meet
I want a budget that is	Flexible	Itemized	Categorized

2- TIME AND COST			
Time a week I can spend on my budget	10 minutes	Under an hour	Under two hours
I want a one off setup time	As short as possible	Under an hour	Anything
I want a budget that costs	Nothing	One-time fee	Ongoing cost

3- KNOWLEDGE			
My math level/tolerance	I hate math	I don't mind math	I'm a math guru
I understand how to use a budget	Not at all	Basic knowledge	In-depth knowledge
I want to know where my money goes	Not at all	Neutral	Definitely
I want to budget	Not at all	Somewhat	Definitely

4- FUTURE PLANNING			
I am saving for	Retirement	Investing	Goals
I want a budget for	Short term	Long term	Don't know
I have these types of debt	Car loan	Student loan	Other debt
I have these types of debt	Credit card	Layby/hire purchase	Personal loan

5- TECHNOLOGY			
Technology and I are	Enemies	Acquaintances	Friends
I want to do my budget	On paper	On the computer	On my phone
I want to sync my budget to	Other tech items	Social media	Nothing!

6- SPENDING HABITS			
When I spend money I use	Mostly cash	Mostly card	Both
When I spend money it's	Spontaneous	Planned	Both
When I see something I really want I	Can walk away	Have to buy it	Different each day
At the end of the week I	Have money left	Am always broke	Different each week

Budget 3: Cash

The flip side of the coin is the Cash budget. If you use your credit card way more than you should, and end up spending far more money than you actually have, then the cash budget could be the way forward. Internet banking has made controlling your finances electronically super easy, and they are available to you at any time, night or day. However, this means you can also spend your money night and day!

Here's how the process works:

The cash budget eliminates mindless card-based spending by getting rid of credit and debit cards for personal use and focusing on cash only. It relies on you leaving your cards at home and only spending the money you actually have in your pocket each week. You need to work out what your spending amount will be, after bills and weekly expenditures are subtracted from your income. You then simply withdraw this amount in cash, and spend only that for the week.

The cash budget is similar to the envelope budget in that it eliminates card spending. However, the envelope budget takes it a step further, and creates a cash system for every area of your life. The cash budget is a simpler form. Most of the money we spend without thought is not on necessities, but on frivolities. You can continue to pay for bills, groceries, and petrol with a card, but use cash only for your personal spending, if this suits more.

Having cash for your spending money is a constant reminder on how much you have left, and if you can afford an item. It also encourages mindfulness when spending, and a deeper understanding of what you throw your money at each week.

1. Complete the 10-step budgeting process and work out how much money you have each week after direct debits and regular bill payments such as rent.

2. Include regular expenses you pay for by card, such as groceries and bills, as part of your budget.

3. Stash all your cards somewhere safe, but hard to access. Keep one card out only, and use this to pay for your regular expenses.

4. Withdraw your remaining amount in cash for the week. This is your spending money.

5. Spend only this for the week and DO NOT allow yourself to use your card.

6. If you want to save for a big item, withdraw less cash and put the remainder aside in a savings account until your goal is reached.

Remember that cash-based spending is not necessarily spending only cash, but is the absence of 'credit': money that you do not have, and have to pay back at a later date. You can still use debit cards that have your pay on them. You just can't use credit cards.

Once your weekly pay has gone from your debit card, you can no longer spend any money. Meaning no debt, and much more awareness of how you are spending your money. This is why the cash-based budget uses card for direct debits, bills, and regular payments, but uses cash for your spending money. It is a lot easier to see how much you've spent, and how much you've got left when using cash.

If you transfer your bill money to a separate account, it can roll over until needed without being 'accidentally' used for other things. You then withdraw your spending amount and the money left in your account is for regular expenses such as groceries and petrol. Need more money one week? It has to come from your spending money. Now you're thinking more carefully about those groceries, aren't you!

Cash based spending	(no credit cards)
Current income per week	$850
Direct debits and bills- transferred to separate account till needed	$500
Regular card expenses such as petrol and groceries- stay in your main account	$220
Cash for spending (or saving)- withdrawn in cash or transferred to a debit card	$130

Pros:

- You can't just hand over a credit card with all that invisible money on it.
- You really have to think about each purchase. This makes you more keyed into your spending and encourages mindfulness.
- You are less likely to be charged bank or credit card fees for being overdrawn or making late payments.
- You can never spend more than you have on unnecessary items.

Cons:

- It can be hard, especially when starting out, not to resort to card-based spending.
- You have to get money out from an ATM each week.
- You tend to add unnecessary purchases into your grocery and petrol buys, to avoid having to spend your minimal cash.

Tips and Tricks:

Set yourself a goal on how long you can last without using a credit card for personal spending, and make yourself accountable by letting people know on social media, or telling a couple of friends who will encourage you.

If you can't get used to not paying on card for things, load your spending money onto a debit card each week and use that. This eliminates the need to go to an ATM, and also lets you easily roll unspent money over to the next pay period. It's not as visually effective though…

Attributes for Cash Budget

1- BUDGET TYPE			
My budget should have	Pictures & Graphs	Figures & Facts	Both
My budget should be	Colour	Black and White	Both
This budget is for	Just me	My family	Other
I like budgets that are	Traditional	Non-traditional	New
I want a budget that's	Simple	Neutral	Complex
I want my budget to focus on	Goals	Savings	Making ends meet
I want a budget that is	Flexible	Itemized	Categorized

2- TIME AND COST			
Time a week I can spend on my budget	10 minutes	Under an hour	Under two hours
I want a one off setup time	As short as possible	Under an hour	Anything
I want a budget that costs	Nothing	One-time fee	Ongoing cost

3- KNOWLEDGE			
My math level/tolerance	I hate math	I don't mind math	I'm a math guru
I understand how to use a budget	Not at all	Basic knowledge	In-depth knowledge
I want to know where my money goes	Not at all	Neutral	Definitely
I want to budget	Not at all	Somewhat	Definitely

4- FUTURE PLANNING			
I am saving for	Retirement	Investing	Goals
I want a budget for	Short term	Long term	Don't know
I have these types of debt	Car loan	Student loan	Other debt
I have these types of debt	Credit card	Layby/hire purchase	Personal loan

5- TECHNOLOGY			
Technology and I are	Enemies	Acquaintances	Friends
I want to do my budget	On paper	On the computer	On my phone
I want to sync my budget to	Other tech items	Social media	Nothing!

6- SPENDING HABITS			
When I spend money I use	Mostly cash	Mostly card	Both
When I spend money it's	Spontaneous	Planned	Both
When I see something I really want I	Can walk away	Have to buy it	Different each day
At the end of the week I	Have money left	Am always broke	Different each week

Budget 4: Percentage

People who want a simpler way of looking at budgeting may do well with this one. You simply split your total income amount into percentages. For example: $800 income a week could be split into 50% ($400) needs, 30% ($240) wants, and 20% ($160) savings.

Here's how the process works:

You can split your percentage any way you like depending on how much you want to save, how much of your pay needs to go towards needs, and whether you want to maintain your lifestyle and spending the way it currently is. You might do 60% needs, 30% savings and 10% wants.

It is literally as simple and as personal as you need it to be.

1. Work out how much income you currently make.

2. Decide what percentage you want to spend on different areas. You might only choose needs, wants, and savings. You might be much more specific and choose bills, ongoing expenses, spending, savings, investing. This part is much easier if you've completed the 10-step budgeting process in *Chapter 3,* but ultimately it's up to you if you do or not.

3. At the beginning of each pay cycle, split your money according to the percentage allocated them. It doesn't matter if you do this with cash or over accounts, as long as it is split.

4. Only spend the amount allocated for each area.

5. Get rid of credit cards where you can, or make sure you allocate the money you spend on them to their appropriate percentages.

6. Review if you are finding there is too much/too little in an area consistently.

The graph below shows 3 different ways you could split your fortnightly income using the percentage budget. Some have large percentages for needs, others are focused on savings. All of them cater to different peoples' lives, and are sustainable for the long term.

Percentage Budget

Income	$1000	$1000	$1000	$1000
Needs	50% - $500	60% - $600	70% - $700	90% - $900
Savings	30% - $300	25% - $250	5% - $50	5% - $50
Wants	20% - $200	15% - $150	25% - $250	5% - $50

The beauty of the percentage budget is its ease of use. If you set your percentages and then find they are not working, it is only a matter of a quick reshuffle to alter them for the following fortnight. It is simple, fast and functional. Gotta love that!

Pros:

- It is fast and simple to set up.
- You don't have to allocate money to every item or even category, just broad percentages. This allows you more flexibility with your spending.
- You don't have to spend time entering data into your budget every week.

- You only need to know your income to set up your budget and a broad idea of the percentages.
- It doesn't matter if your income changes every week.

Cons:

- If you spend money somewhere that covers more than one category, you have to balance that at the end of the day
- It can be hard to differentiate between the wants and needs when it comes to things such as groceries and clothes.
- You don't get as fine a grasp of what you spend your money on as with itemized budgets.
- There aren't apparent goals with this budget, so it is easy to lose momentum and give up.

Tips and Tricks:

Set up 3 debit cards which link to your needs, wants, and savings accounts. Load these cards with the percentage of your income you have decided on, and use them when making purchases. Not only does this mean you can't spend more than you have in each category, it gives you an instant record of your spending.

Attributes for Percentage Budget

1- BUDGET TYPE			
My budget should have	Pictures & Graphs	Figures & Facts	Both
My budget should be	Colour	Black and White	Both
This budget is for	Just me	My family	Other
I like budgets that are	Traditional	Non-traditional	New
I want a budget that's	Simple	Neutral	Complex
I want my budget to focus on	Goals	Savings	Making ends meet
I want a budget that is	Flexible	Itemized	Categorized

2- TIME AND COST			
Time a week I can spend on my budget	10 minutes	Under an hour	Under two hours
I want a one off setup time	As short as possible	Under an hour	Anything
I want a budget that costs	Nothing	One-time fee	Ongoing cost

3- KNOWLEDGE			
My math level/tolerance	I hate math	I don't mind math	I'm a math guru
I understand how to use a budget	Not at all	Basic knowledge	In-depth knowledge
I want to know where my money goes	Not at all	Neutral	Definitely
I want to budget	Not at all	Somewhat	Definitely

4- FUTURE PLANNING			
I am saving for	Retirement	Investing	Goals
I want a budget for	Short term	Long term	Don't know
I have these types of debt	Car loan	Student loan	Other debt
I have these types of debt	Credit card	Layby/hire purchase	Personal loan

5- TECHNOLOGY			
Technology and I are	Enemies	Acquaintances	Friends
I want to do my budget	On paper	On the computer	On my phone
I want to sync my budget to	Other tech items	Social media	Nothing!

6- SPENDING HABITS			
When I spend money I use	Mostly cash	Mostly card	Both
When I spend money it's	Spontaneous	Planned	Both
When I see something I really want I	Can walk away	Have to buy it	Different each day
At the end of the week I	Have money left	Am always broke	Different each week

Budget 5: 3-Step

Similar to the percentage budget is the 3-Step budget. It is simple, fast to set up, and easy to follow. It doesn't take a lot of time each week and allows you a lot of flexibility with your spending - to a certain degree.

Here's how the process works:

1. Get rid of credit cards. All of them. Even your emergency one.
2. Set aside 20% of your income for savings. Put this into a separate account and don't touch it, until it reaches an amount where it can be used to invest, pay debt, or to pay for your goals.
3. Use the remaining 80% to pay for your day-to-day expenses, spending money, and bills.

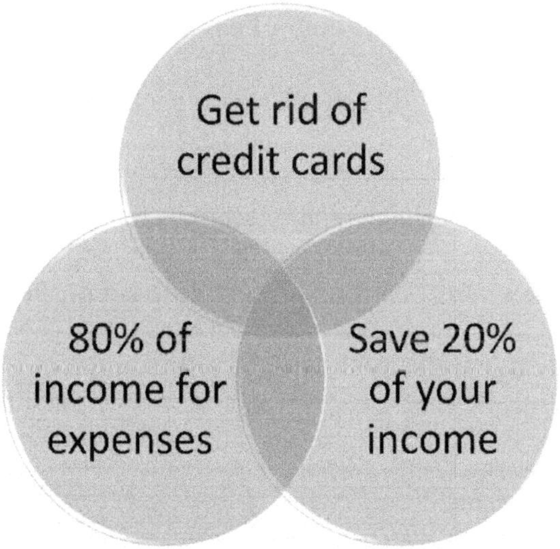

It is literally that simple. Of course, you still have to have the ability to stick to it, which may be harder than you think. If you currently rely on your credit card as a backup, or use it to pay for everything and pay it off when you can, it's going to be a massive change. If you don't really use credit cards, then this budget should be relatively easy for you to assimilate.

The 3-Step budget works well because it gets rid of temptation and only allows you to spend the money you actually have. Yes, you have a lot of freedom in how you spend that money, but it has to be there for you to use it. And this is what makes it work.

It also allows for a good amount of saving to happen, which is perfect if you need to pay off debt, save for a house deposit, or realise your goal of traveling the world.

Pros:

- Simple to use and understand
- Fast to set up and takes very little time after that
- Allows for a good amount of saving
- Gives you flexibility in what you spend your money on every week
- Is not as restrictive as many budgets
- Abolishes credit card debt by getting rid of them altogether.
- Can change each week with your income.

Cons:

- Can be hard to adapt to if you use your credit card a lot.
- You miss out on credit card points and offers.
- Doesn't force you to save money for bills and expenses, so you could easily get into trouble if your bills appear all at once.

- Doesn't give you much of an insight into your spending habits.
- No credit card as a backup in emergencies.
- No good if you're struggling to make ends meet.

Tips and Tricks:

Don't just hide your credit cards, close the accounts or give your cards to someone you trust to hold onto. For this budget to work you need to stop using credit altogether. Make your savings account in a different bank with no Internet banking or debit card. This means you actually have to make it to a bank in trading hours to access those savings. Chances are if you make that much of an effort, you've reached your goal rather than found something awesome on an infomercial. Make sure you have some money left over each week from your 80%, so if a big bill comes in, you're not struggling to find money.

Attributes for 3 step Budget

1- BUDGET TYPE			
My budget should have	Pictures & Graphs	Figures & Facts	Both
My budget should be	Colour	Black and White	Both
This budget is for	Just me	My family	Other
I like budgets that are	Traditional	Non-traditional	New
I want a budget that's	Simple	Neutral	Complex
I want my budget to focus on	Goals	Savings	Making ends meet
I want a budget that is	Flexible	Itemized	Categorized

2- TIME AND COST			
Time a week I can spend on my budget	10 minutes	Under an hour	Under two hours
I want a one off setup time	As short as possible	Under an hour	Anything
I want a budget that costs	Nothing	One-time fee	Ongoing cost

3- KNOWLEDGE			
My math level/tolerance	I hate math	I don't mind math	I'm a math guru
I understand how to use a budget	Not at all	Basic knowledge	In-depth knowledge
I want to know where my money goes	Not at all	Neutral	Definitely
I want to budget	Not at all	Somewhat	Definitely

4- FUTURE PLANNING			
I am saving for	Retirement	Investing	Goals
I want a budget for	Short term	Long term	Don't know
I have these types of debt	Car loan	Student loan	Other debt
I have these types of debt	Credit card	Layby/hire purchase	Personal loan

5- TECHNOLOGY			
Technology and I are	Enemies	Acquaintances	Friends
I want to do my budget	On paper	On the computer	On my phone
I want to sync my budget to	Other tech items	Social media	Nothing!

6- SPENDING HABITS			
When I spend money I use	Mostly cash	Mostly card	Both
When I spend money it's	Spontaneous	Planned	Both
When I see something I really want I	Can walk away	Have to buy it	Different each day
At the end of the week I	Have money left	Am always broke	Different each week

Recap:

- Bucket list budget: Focusing on achieving goals, rather than keeping track of your spending. Can be used to reach large or small goals, over short or long periods.

- Cashless budget: Works to reduce spending by removing cash from your life. Also easier to keep track of what you spend, as it is all on your bank statement.

- Cash budget: Helps you minimize credit card debt and the spending of money you don't have, by removing all credit and debit cards for spending. You withdraw only the cash you have for the coming week.

- Percentage budget: Splits your total income into percentages for large areas such as expenses, spending and savings.

- 3-Step budget: Removes credit cards, sets aside 20% for savings, and allows you freedom to spend the remaining 80% on everything else.

Don't forget you can download worksheets for all the different budgets on our website[25]. Now that you've seen how non-traditional budgets work, jump into *Chapter 10: There's an App for That! Technology and Budgets*. Get tips for how to save money, meet goals, and keep track of your money on the go - without the hoopla of a paper budget.

---

[25] http://www.how2without.com/bonus-materials/bbdd-pdf-workbook/

CHAPTER 10:
THERE'S AN APP FOR THAT! TECHNOLOGY AND BUDGETS

Budgeting apps are filling the void between the math-heavy budgets we know and hate, and people's time-poor, instant success lifestyles. They have been created to be simpler, faster, and more interactive than any paper budget around.

Apps are familiar, can be used on the go, and often don't seem like a chore. And smart phones are something most of us not only carry around everywhere, but already use for a multitude of different tasks.

Top budgeting apps sync with your bank accounts (more on this later), create data on your spending, bills, and ongoing expenses, and create an individual budget for you, without you breaking a sweat.

Some only do specific things like splitting a bill, or tracking your direct debits, but others are truly amazing. They can pull data from scanned receipts, automatically categorize expenses, and provide you with balances and weekly spend amounts. You can even share your goals with your mates. It's pretty incredible.

I have listed my favourite apps, and some of their best points, below. But apps, like technology in general, are constantly changing. Because of this, my line-up will too. Upgrades don't always make an app better, some apps don't change with the times, and more apps appear on the scene every day.

To grab yourself an up-to-date and more comprehensive PDF, hit my website[26] for a free download that covers: What the app provides, how

[26] http://www.how2without.com/bonus-materials/top-finance-apps-for-ios-and-android/

they work, their security settings and guarantees, the initial and ongoing costs, and reviews from users - not the companies. All this information is invaluable in making an informed decision about any risks involved, and what will work for you in the long run.

BillGuard - by Prosper

BillGuard organizes all the activity and balances on your credit cards, debit cards, and bank accounts into one Smart Inbox. Tracks your spending and credit, and alerts you to suspicious activity that your bank missed. BillGuard also has the most advanced ID theft protection ever created.

Budgt

This clever app will create a new budget for you every day, based on how much you've already spent during the month. By making you aware of how much you can afford each day, BUDGT allows for easy savings. Minimalistic, clean take on a zero sum budget.

Expensify

Acknowledged by the tech community as the best app for expense reporting, Expensify takes the time, paper, and headaches out of expense reports. Lets you photograph, categorize, and tag receipts, and add to an expense report if necessary. You can also invoice clients with it.

Good Budget (Easy Envelope Budgeting Aid)

One of the leading expense and budget trackers; it allows you to proactively plan finances ahead of time with the Envelope system of budgeting. Allows you to sync and share your budget with family members, analyse expenses, and plan your finances.

Level Money

This easy to set up app provides you with your Spendable - or safe to spend number - for the day, week, and month. Gives you the ability to track your spending habits by merchant and category, and personalize your spending and saving goals.

Mint

Perhaps the most well-known budgeting app, Mint helps you spend smarter, and save more. Easily pulls all your accounts, cards and investments into one place so you can track your spending, create a budget, receive bill reminders, and get customized tips for reducing fees and saving money.

Mvelopes

Built upon the envelope budgeting approach, Mvelopes helps you categorize your spending, plan your budget ahead of time, and track how much money you have left throughout the month. You can capture receipts from your phone and attach them to purchases, and assign transactions to expense envelopes.

Personal Capital

Combines award-winning online financial tools with licensed financial planners to help you understand, manage, and grow your net worth. Has interactive cash flow tools to help you create and follow a budget, and can also track your investments and net worth.

Pocketbook

Australian based, this is one of the top-rated budgeting apps worldwide, and provides 'real time' health checks on your finances, budgeting tools, and bill detection. Can be used to lodge your tax return, and syncs to your bank accounts.

Pocket Expense

Brings all your financial accounts together, categorizes your transactions, tracks all your bills, lets you set budgets, and helps you achieve your savings goals. It supports multiple budgets, and shows statistics for a day, week, month, or year.

Spendbook

Its elegant and uniquely designed user interface makes for a stunning app packed with features. Spendbook tracks your expenses, and has intuitive charts that break them down and show them on a calendar. You can also set up and manage multiple accounts, and customize categories.

Spendee

A beautifully designed app with a sleek, simple layout, that syncs in real time across all devices. You can create specific wallets for different purposes, and share them with your family and friends. Also has the ability to add your transactions to different budgets, and choose a location where each purchase took place.

TrackmySPEND

This easy-to-use app lets you track actual spending against a budget or salary, or against a spending period or pay period. You can mark expenses as a want or need, and create favourites for frequent expenses.

Wallet - Budget Tracker

A comprehensive income and expenses tracker with reliable cloud synchronization, high safety, and the unique option to manage your home finance (balance, cash flow, shopping lists, budgets, debts, warranties etc.) together with your partner or family.

Wally

A lifestyle app that treats expenses as experiences, Wally shows you where you stand financially compared to people like you. It tells you where, why, on what, and with who you spend money, so you know exactly where your money goes, and notifies users when a bill is due, or if they've reached a goal.

YNAB (You Need a Budget)

YNAB is a powerful methodology coupled with award-winning software that allows you to sync the app across all devices, move money easily between categories, and enter transactions on the go. Works offline and doesn't sync to your bank account, but you can check category balances before making a purchase.

* * *

Like written budgets, apps only make a difference if you use them consistently. No budgeting app will be foolproof if you only use it now and then, or don't provide it with the relevant data.

There are many different apps to choose from that can help you create a great budget and stick to it, you just have to narrow them down to the one that suits you best! Remember, this is just a few of the best ones currently. For an up-to-date list, and a stack more info, hit my website[27] for a free PDF download.

What's the downside? Budgeting apps work by gathering all your bank information and creating a snapshot of your finances. To do this, some apps need you to provide them with sensitive bank details, such as credit card numbers and account passwords. It is this that worries banks and users alike. Always, always, check current data on an app

[27] http://www.how2without.com/bonus-materials/top-finance-apps-for-ios-and-android/

before allowing it access to your banking information. The last thing you need is for all your sensitive information to be available to others.

The good news is that most apps are read-only. This means that you can view the information within the app, but you cannot alter it. You, the app, or third parties are unable to make purchases or pay bills. Withdrawals, transfers, or account changes have to be made through your bank's operating system, and simply cannot be done in the app. Some apps like Mint have add-on apps that you can use to pay bills. I would worry more about these than the actual budgeting app itself…

Some banks and card networks say in the event of a breach; zero-liability protection would cover any fraudulent charges. Other banks policies cover both debit and credit cards, and say app use has no impact on card protections. Most, however, say you are opening yourself up for fraud, and that giving your information to a third party app voids any responsibility the bank may have had. This is something you would need to work out with your own bank.

There is an excellent article on app safety at creditcards.com[28] which is worth a read, but the bottom line is this: you are more likely to lose information through a spam-phishing email, or a dodgy website, than through use of an app. Not to mention carrying your credit card around in your pocket every day…

Experts believe the greatest risk when using a budgeting app is not from the app itself, but rather the fact that all that information is in one handy location on your phone, should it ever be lost or stolen. Always make sure you have not only a pin number on your phone, but that the app you choose has a bomb-proof log-in procedure.

App developers also know how important it is to keep your information safe, and any app worth its salt has excellent encryption,

---

[28] http://www.creditcards.com/credit-card-news/7-tips-using-budget-apps-safely-1282.php

on par with those a bank uses. This means that it would be just as hard for a hacker to access your personal information from the app as it would be from your bank's Internet banking page.

Here are some of the things you can do to keep safe when using a budgeting app:

1. Confirm the validity of an app before downloading, as well as its security ratings and reviews.

2. Only use an app at a level that you are comfortable with. If you're not good with technology and online security, then this probably isn't the best place to learn.

3. Always protect yourself with a password. Not the one you've had since high school. A good one with capitals, symbols, and no links to your personal life. You can even set it up with a remote wipe capability, which clears your device if lost or stolen. Cool!

4. Don't use auto logins. Ever. Always set up an app so you have to use a password or pin when you open it. Every. Single. Time.

5. Use anti-virus software on your phone. We all use it on our home computers, and yet our phones, which we use just as much, aren't similarly protected.

6. Pay attention to alerts your budgeting apps give. They help track fraudulent behaviour, and if you can catch it quick, then the bank will often cover you, not to mention it will stop it happening again.

7. Try not to use public Wi-Fi. Use your phone's data or your home Wi-Fi, as it is more secure. If you do use your app in

pubic, make sure your phone can't be seen by anyone sitting close, and remember to log off as soon as you're finished.

8. Never click on pop up advertising within an app. EVER.

9. Never give out your bank details to anyone contacting you from the app via phone or email. Apps are read only, but it means criminals who do hack in can read your information too, and use it to reference your spending or accounts, tricking you into giving out your details.

10. Every time your app updates, make sure the security settings are still high, and in place.

If any (or all) of this is making you feel uncomfortable and a little bit queasy, don't worry. You can still use online apps that don't need access to any of your bank details, you just have to enter all your expenses manually instead of the app doing all the dirty work for you. It might be more labour intensive, but at least you can sleep at night knowing no one but you is looking at your bank details.

I believe the reward of using budgeting apps outweigh the risks, but that is my personal opinion. You need to be smart about them, and take precautions, but if you aren't comfortable with the idea of your information being online, then don't do it!

I just figure with all the bills I pay online, and all the purchases I make on random websites, my information is already out there. My budgeting app is probably the safest aspect of my online world! Like everything though, the choice is yours. Just make sure you make an informed and conscious decision about the best option for you, your lifestyle, and your finances.

Attributes for App Based Budgets

1- BUDGET TYPE			
My budget should have	Pictures & Graphs	Figures & Facts	Both
My budget should be	Colour	Black and White	Both
This budget is for	Just me	My family	Other
I like budgets that are	Traditional	Non-traditional	New
I want a budget that's	Simple	Neutral	Complex
I want my budget to focus on	Goals	Savings	Making ends meet
I want a budget that is	Flexible	Itemized	Categorized

2- TIME AND COST			
Time a week I can spend on my budget	10 minutes	Under an hour	Under two hours
I want a one off setup time	As short as possible	Under an hour	Anything
I want a budget that costs	Nothing	One-time fee	Ongoing cost

3- KNOWLEDGE			
My math level/tolerance	I hate math	I don't mind math	I'm a math guru
I understand how to use a budget	Not at all	Basic knowledge	In-depth knowledge
I want to know where my money goes	Not at all	Neutral	Definitely
I want to budget	Not at all	Somewhat	Definitely

4- FUTURE PLANNING			
I am saving for	Retirement	Investing	Goals
I want a budget for	Short term	Long term	Don't know
I have these types of debt	Car loan	Student loan	Other debt
I have these types of debt	Credit card	Layby/hire purchase	Personal loan

5- TECHNOLOGY			
Technology and I are	Enemies	Acquaintances	Friends
I want to do my budget	On paper	On the computer	On my phone
I want to sync my budget to	Other tech items	Social media	Nothing!

6- SPENDING HABITS			
When I spend money I use	Mostly cash	Mostly card	Both
When I spend money it's	Spontaneous	Planned	Both
When I see something I really want I	Can walk away	Have to buy it	Different each day
At the end of the week I	Have money left	Am always broke	Different each week

Recap:

- Apps should simplify your life, not complicate it.
- Apps can save time by sorting through your finances in a fraction of the time you could.
- If an app is accessing your bank accounts, make sure it has a secure encryption and excellent reviews and security settings.
- Apps are brilliant for people on the go, as the technology they use is always with us.
- Budgeting apps each offer different things. Choose one that best fits with you and your lifestyle.

What's next? A research report[29] conducted by Forrester Research provides some clues on what else might be ahead for banking apps. According to the report, several European bank apps allow users to photograph a bill to initiate a payment, and some also offer secure messaging with advisors in-app. How crazy is that? It is an ever-changing world.

To get the full list on all the best apps, head to our website[30] where you can download a stack of up-to-date information on a range of different apps. For some more wild ideas, check out *Chapter 11: F for Finance. Unusual Budgets from a Mad Mind.*

---

[29] https://www.forrester.com/report/The+State+Of+Mobile+Banking+2014/-/E-RES107321

[30] http://www.how2without.com/bonus-materials/top-finance-apps-for-ios-and-android/

CHAPTER II:

F FOR FINANCE. UNUSUAL BUDGETS FROM A MAD MIND

Not every budget suits every person. Hopefully you've made that distinction by now. But what if no budget suits you? Welcome to the club! I really struggled with picking a budget. Some were too restrictive, some had too many numbers, and some not enough. I got so frustrated, not to mention annoyed with myself, for jumping from one budget to another. Nothing was working! So I created a couple of 'new' budgets, especially for us crazies…

Budget 1: Choose your own adventure

A few years back, yet another 'test your brain' questionnaire came across my Facebook feed. As always it came back, 'your brain is equal across all fields.' Never done, or heard of these tests? Here's a quick rundown.

There are many different forms of this test. Some show the 4 ways of learning - Spatial/Visual learning, Tactile/Kinetic learning, Auditory learning, and Logical learning. Others show whether you use mostly the left (rational) or right (creative) side of your brain. Whatever the test, the bottom line is, everyone's brain functions in a different way.

If you've never done one of these tests I highly recommend them. It will help you understand which area of your brain is the most dominant, how you learn, and why you do the things you do.

No matter which test I do, mine always comes out almost equal between all parts. What does this mean? I learn equally well visually and kinetically as I do through auditory and logical learning. I am equally creative and rational.

While this may seem wonderful, most of the learning we do in life is either visual or auditory (reading or listening). I can handle this, but I get bored easily. I need colour, graphs and pictures. I need to manipulate objects and see how they work. I need change, or it's all just too…blah.

I mean, I love to read, but if you ask me at the end of the book what a character looks like I could tell you in detail. I don't need to see a picture of them. I create images in my mind of the people and places I read about. I'm not just seeing words on a page; I'm seeing them in my imagination. I always think they cast people wrong when a book gets made into a movie!

Unfortunately, finance does not lend itself to image creation. It's just not interesting enough for most people. So it's best to create our budgets the way we learn and understand knowledge from the outset. And then it all slid into place. Most budgets don't suit me because they only focus on one area. They are either visual with lots of pie charts and graphs, or they are very logical with lots of numbers and equations.

Apps cover the most learning styles in budgeting, as they are tactile, visual, and logical. Most people are generally more heavily skewed towards one way of learning, which makes it much easier to pick a budget that suits your personality. If, however you're like me, and your brain is evenly split, or you just can't find a budget that works for you, then you might be better off choosing your own adventure.

Here's how the process works:

I use money mindfulness in my everyday life. This, to me, is my most important budgeting feature. I also have a traditional category budget, which I use a few times a year. It shows me what my expenses are, my savings, and my spare cash in relation to my income. I also use a bucket list budget to help me achieve my savings goals. These three very different ways of budgeting form my 'choose your own adventure' budget, and ensure that I actually stick to something and meet my goals.

Work out what components of the different budgeting formats work for you, and then combine them to create your ultimate budget. Remember that these should work together, not independently of each other. Choosing your own budget combinations may take a little longer than just following a stock budget, but because they work with you as an individual, you'll find them easier to stick with and incorporate into your life.

This means that your goals will be met quicker, and your finances will be a lot healthier. Once you've created a budget that suits your personality, and plays to your strengths instead of your weaknesses, you'll be away. Every budget should suit the individual using it, not the masses, so make your budget as unique as you are!

1. Go through *Chapter 13* and see if you can narrow down a single budget. Use the forms to help you understand what type of budget best suits you and your personality.

2. If none of the standard budgets suit, then create your own budget, using the best components from each budget. Each combination should work together with the others to create your ultimate budget.

3. Set up your budget using the specific steps involved for each individual budget you've chosen (where applicable).

4. Feel free to swap components out when they are not working and try others.

Choose Your Own Adventure

Budget type	Areas covered	When/how often is use	Specific steps
Mindfulness	Money mindfulness	Every day	Write notes to remind myself. Tell a friend when shopping together. Buy a purse with a lock. Work on thinking, acting and benefiting from being mindful.
Pocketbook App	Tracking my card-based spending	Once a week- 25 mins	Set up app. At end of each week tally card spending. Allocate to categories and ensure too much is not being spent. Take note if need to spend less next week.
Category Budget	Rough idea of finances for the year	4 times a year/ 2 hrs	Set up a simple category budget that shows how much income we make, how much we can spend and save in each area. Review every 3 months and change when necessary.
Bucket list	Help achieve ongoing goals	Once a week- 5 mins	Set up a chart with big and small goals. Make some short term and others long term. Make sure they are things I really want and wouldn't normally make money for.
Notes:			

Pros:

- You get to create a budget that suits you specifically, no one else.
- You will have more success sticking to your budget and meeting your goals with a budget you are comfortable with.
- It is more likely to become something you do long-term, rather than a passing fad, if it fits into your life comfortably.

Cons:

- People may struggle with not having one neat and precise budget laid out for them.
- It is easy to choose all the simple budgeting components, not because they work for you, but because you want to avoid knowing what you actually spend, or becoming accountable for your money.

- It can take time to find components that will work for you long term.

Tips and Tricks:

Complete the checklists I've included in the workbook[31], as these will give you an instant idea of what components are going to work best for you. Give each combination a chance to work before swapping it out for something new. Create a chart showing how each area will influence and help the other areas. Ensure every area of your financial life is covered.

There is no attributes graph for the *Choose Your Own Adventure* budget as you can make it as unique as you like. It can encompass all the attributes you like the most if set up correctly.

---

[31] http://www.how2without.com/bonus-materials/bbdd-pdf-workbook/

Budget 2: Spend and save

Spend and save is a new, innovative budget from yours truly, which simplifies how you spend and save money by minimizing the thought process surrounding it. It's really simple. If you've spent it, you have to save it.

Here's how the process works:

Start by getting rid of any credit cards you may have, or at the very least hiding them in a dark closet. This budget will <u>not</u> work with credit. Okay, say you earn $750 a week. Instead of separating that money out into different categories and compartments you:

1. Pay whatever bills have come in.
2. Buy groceries, fuel, and any other day-to-day expenses.
3. Set aside money to cover direct debits such as rent, phone, and subscriptions.
4. Calculate the money you have left. This amount will be different every week, so don't panic.
5. Once you have your amount, spend it and save it. You can either work on a 1:1 ratio or a 1:2 ratio, or if you are feeling really lazy, a 1:3 ratio. What does this mean? If you have $100 left over at the end of the week, you would spend $50 and save $50 (1:1). Or spend $67 and save $34 (1:2). Or (you lazy thing, you) spend $75 and save $25 (1:3).

How much you spend and save will depend entirely on you. It may even change week to week, although I think this makes it a bit harder to stick to. Having a specific spend and save ratio means you save money even when spending it. It also encourages you to think carefully about what you spend, as each dollar spent has a knock on effect on how much you need to save.

Some weeks, you might not spend much. Let's use that $100 as an example again. You spend $30 and are on a 1:2 savings ratio, which means you need to save $15. You have $55 left over. Next week rolls around and you have $140 left over to spend, plus your remaining $55, making $195. Using your 1:2 ratio, this would give you a spend amount of $130 with savings of $65.

If you want to buy a big item, you can continue to roll over your spending money week to week. Just remember that when you do finally spend it, you have to add to your savings as well.

If you look at the 3 graphs below you can see how the ratios might work. We have used the same amount of money for all the other expenses portrayed, only the spending and saving portions have been altered to reflect the ratios. You may spend and save more or less than this, it is just an example.

1:1 RATIO

1:2 RATIO

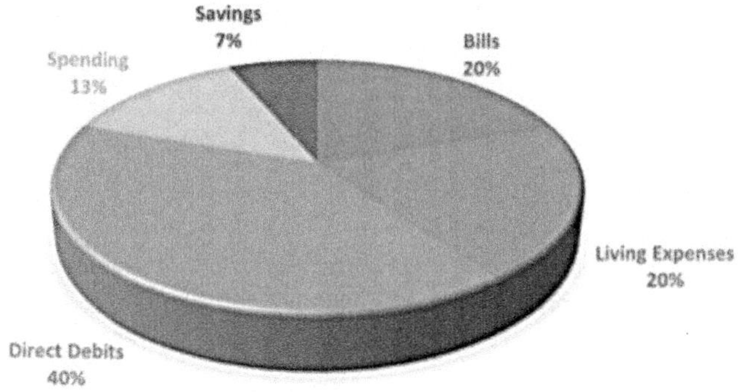

1:3 RATIO

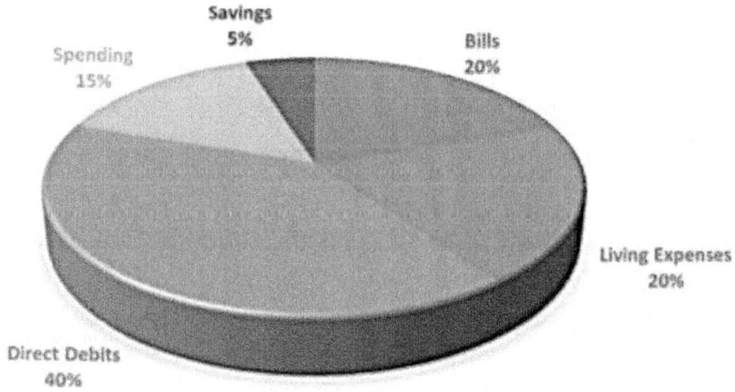

There is a catch though (of course). If you have accumulated $500 to buy a new surfboard and spend it all without adding to your savings, you then can't spend a cent until you've made it up. That's $250 you have to add to your savings on a 1:2 ratio, before you can even buy a coffee! So be mindful of what you spend. Here's a cheat sheet to make it easy to work out your ratios.

SPEND AND SAVE RATIOS

SPEND AMOUNT	1:1 SAVE RATIO	1:2 SAVE RATIO	1:3 SAVE RATIO
$10	$10	$5	$3.50
$15	$15	$7.50	$5
$20	$20	$10	$6.50
$25	$25	$12.50	$8.50
$30	$30	$15	$10
$50	$50	$25	$16.50
$75	$75	$37.50	$25
$100	$100	$50	$33.50
$125	$125	$62.50	$41.50
$150	$150	$75	$50
$175	$175	$87.50	$58.50
$200	$200	$100	$66.50
$250	$250	$125	$83.50
$500	$500	$250	$166.50
$1000	$1000	$500	$333.50

I love this budget so much because spending suddenly becomes a whole lot more guilt-free. Because every time you're spending, you're saving too. How awesome is that? I mean, shopping, without feeling bad about it? Bring it on!

Pros:

- You don't have to worry if your income fluctuates over time, as your spend amount is calculated fresh each week.
- You don't have to plan ahead for bills - you can just pay them as they come in.
- You can pick a savings ratio based on the goals you want to achieve, and how much you normally spend week to week.
- You don't have to set up a budget and spend time entering all your transactions. You only have to keep track of your total spend, so you can work out your savings amount.

- Great for people who prefer to live day to day instead of budgeting for the future.
- Savings amounts will grow really fast, especially on a 1:1 ratio, which is great if you're saving for a house or overseas travel.
- It encourages mindful spending, as whatever you spend has to be matched with a save.

Cons:

- If you have a big bill come in, or encounter an emergency situation, the only way you can finance it is by using your savings.
- Some people will not have the willpower to add to savings on any sort of ratio with their spending.
- This budget will not help you minimize day-to-day expenses.
- People who are struggling to make ends meet will not have enough spare cash to save at this level.

Tips and Tricks:

Set up 2 accounts, one for savings and one for spending. Do all your spending from this account, not with cash. This way you'll always have a record of your spending without having to tally receipts, and you will be less likely to fritter it away on small items such as coffee.

Separate your spending and savings amount into their ratios as soon as you get it. This means whatever money you have in savings is yours to spend. It also stops you 'accidentally on purpose' spending more than the ratio.

If you're on a 1:1 ratio and are struggling or unhappy, drop your ratio down. It is better to save less over a longer period than to save more for a short period and then give up. The same is also true if you find you are rolling money over every week on a 1:3 ratio. Save a bit more and reach your goal sooner. Win-win!

Attributes for Spend and Save Budget

1- BUDGET TYPE			
My budget should have	Pictures & Graphs	Figures & Facts	Both
My budget should be	Colour	Black and White	Both
This budget is for	Just me	My family	Other
I like budgets that are	Traditional	Non-traditional	New
I want a budget that's	Simple	Neutral	Complex
I want my budget to focus on	Goals	Savings	Making ends meet
I want a budget that is	Flexible	Itemized	Categorized

2- TIME AND COST			
Time a week I can spend on my budget	10 minutes	Under an hour	Under two hours
I want a one off setup time	As short as possible	Under an hour	Anything
I want a budget that costs	Nothing	One-time fee	Ongoing cost

3- KNOWLEDGE			
My math level/tolerance	I hate math	I don't mind math	I'm a math guru
I understand how to use a budget	Not at all	Basic knowledge	In-depth knowledge
I want to know where my money goes	Not at all	Neutral	Definitely
I want to budget	Not at all	Somewhat	Definitely

4- FUTURE PLANNING			
I am saving for	Retirement	Investing	Goals
I want a budget for	Short term	Long term	Don't know
I have these types of debt	Car loan	Student loan	Other debt
I have these types of debt	Credit card	Layby/hire purchase	Personal loan

5- TECHNOLOGY			
Technology and I are	Enemies	Acquaintances	Friends
I want to do my budget	On paper	On the computer	On my phone
I want to sync my budget to	Other tech items	Social media	Nothing!

6- SPENDING HABITS			
When I spend money I use	Mostly cash	Mostly card	Both
When I spend money it's	Spontaneous	Planned	Both
When I see something I really want I	Can walk away	Have to buy it	Different each day
At the end of the week I	Have money left	Am always broke	Different each week

Recap:

- Choose your own adventure budget: Combines elements that work best for you, from a range of different budgets.
- Spend and Save budget: Uses a ratio to encourage saving alongside spending.

Fillable graphs are available[32] to help you get started with these unusual budgets. If you've read all the above and still don't think you can budget, or simply don't want to budget, then don't stress. I've got the perfect solution. Don't budget!

Chapter 12: *Non-budgets. Budgets Without the Budgeting* will show you how to get similar results from a couple of non-budgets as from a written budget. Intrigued? You should be!

---

[32] http://www.how2without.com/bonus-materials/bbdd-pdf-workbook/

CHAPTER 12:

NON-BUDGETS: BUDGETS WITHOUT THE BUDGETING

So you really hate budgeting. You hate the idea of it. You hate doing it, and you especially hate sticking to it. What should you do? Don't budget! Practice money mindfulness instead. This technique is the no. 1 reason I'll be able to pay off my mortgage in 10 years instead of 30. Or learn to push yourself and sign up for the boot camp budget. Your bank account will thank you for it!

Budget 1: Money mindfulness.

I first encountered the term money mindfulness while researching for my book *Mortgage Free*[33]. At the time I didn't think much of it. It wasn't what I needed for my book, so I pushed it from my mind. But it has cropped up many times since then, and while I was neck deep in budgeting strategies it struck me - this simple practice is the answer people who suck at budgets need.

You've all heard of yoga, right? One of their key learnings is mindfulness. Mindfulness is calm awareness of one's physical sensations, thoughts, and feelings. In yoga this means being aware of your breathing, your body and your thoughts.

The new adult colouring books that are all the rage right now promote mindfulness. They encourage you to center your thoughts on the calm of colouring and release the stress and madness of the day. Many holistic healers also promote mindfulness as a great way to relieve

[33] http://amzn.to/1NBMTKQ

stress, increase self-awareness, and effectively handle difficult thoughts and feelings.

So what's all this mumbo jumbo got to do with budgeting? Or not budgeting? Mindfulness in regards to our money is a way of being aware of what we spend and is the key to minimizing our spending and maximising our saving. Mindfulness is nothing more than being aware. To be money mindful is to *think* about expenditure, *act* to reduce it, and *benefit* from the results.

Here's how the process works:

A girlfriend asks me out for a day of shopping. We decide to car-pool to the mall to minimize fuel costs. Mindfulness. We shop for a couple of hours and every time I want something I think: *Do I need it?* If I don't need it, but still want it, I think: *"Where would I put it, when would I use it, and can I get it cheaper somewhere else?"* Mindfulness. We head to a café for lunch. I order a massive bowl of nachos (yum!), but I get tap water to go with it instead of paying for a drink. Mindfulness.

These simple things might not seem like they would make a big difference, but if you are using mindfulness in every area of your life, all these little changes become big savings. If you saved $40 from that shopping day, $4 the next day when you decided you could wait for coffee till you got home, $3 to walk the block instead of catching the bus, $15 by renting a DVD instead of going to the movies, and $1 for not upsizing your meal, you would have saved $63 in one week. Times that by 52 and you've got yourself a tidy $3,276 in savings for the year. Not bad for not budgeting.

Being mindful of your money is a fantastic way NOT to budget if you are in a financial position where you would like to save for something, or have a little more left over at the end of the day, without the stress and restrictions of a budget.

It is also great at showing you what you spend money on normally without a second thought, and how you can work on bettering these areas without discarding them altogether. Print a money mindfulness checklist[34] to help you get started.

Like any other learned skill, mindfulness is tricky at first, but the more you do it the easier it becomes, until you don't even realise you're using it. As I said earlier, I currently have a 'choose your own adventure' budget, and money mindfulness plays a huge role in how I interact with money on a day-to-day basis. It's not something I think about, it's a reflex. So much so that when I first came across the term money mindfulness I didn't even click that it was the very thing I already did.

When I was younger I was horrendous with money. It went out as fast as it came in. I don't even really know what I was spending it on, but spend it I did! It never occurred to me to spend only what I was earning (duh!), or that at some point the student loan that was floating my college years would have to be repaid. I went through life completely oblivious to money, and the hole I was digging for myself.

I met my husband when I was 17, and without him I wonder if I would ever be where I am now, helping others with the very thing I was struggling with at the time. He was a saver, not a spender, and his example made me start questioning what I was spending and what I wanted my future to be like. I knew I didn't want to be broke, or in debt, but it is hard to change the habits of a lifetime.

I started small. I got a part-time job flipping burgers after college so I didn't have to use as much of my loan. I started to buy less 'stuff' and put more thought into my purchases. Don't get me wrong, I failed miserably - a lot. But every day I got better at it. It just took perseverance and practice. I paid off my student loan while I worked

[34] http://www.how2without.com/bonus-materials/bbdd-pdf-workbook/

in the UK, using the exchange rate to my advantage, and became debt free for the first time in my adult life. It was a great feeling!

Practicing money mindfulness became second nature to me, and while I still stuff up, spend more than I should, and ignore that little voice of reason from time to time, it has stood me in good stead. I don't budget in the traditional sense of the word, but I finish the week with more money in my pocket than I started it, and I have plans for the future that I know I can achieve. That, to me, is successful budgeting.

Pros:

- Simple way to minimize spending and maximise savings.
- There is no setup involved.
- There is no time invested each week.
- You don't need any knowledge of budgeting.
- Don't need to cut the things you love out of your life.
- Don't need to plan for the future.
- Don't need a steady income source.

Cons:

- Like any other learned skill, mindfulness is tricky at first, but the more you do it the easier it becomes.
- Requires dedication for it to work.
- Need to be willing to make changes.
- Doesn't give you a firm grasp of your finances.
- Doesn't help you save money for the future.

- Won't help you reach goals.

Tips and Tricks:

To be money mindful is to think, act, and benefit. The hard part is learning to think about it. Until it becomes second nature, you can try adding post-it notes to your credit cards and wallet, or buying a lockup or tie up wallet as a way of reminding you to think about your spending.

You can tell friends and family members to remind you if they see you buying without thought, and you can even write on your hand if you know you're hitting the shops. As soon as you've learnt to think, you can work on acting on your thoughts. (-:

Money mindfulness doesn't have an attributes checklist, as it is not a 'true' budget. It doesn't give you any knowledge of what you spend, it doesn't help you save or pay off debt, and it doesn't help you make ends meet. What it does do is make you more conscious of the money you spend every day, so that all of those things are much easier to achieve, if you do decide to budget specifically for them.

It also encourages you not to fritter money away by attaching thought to every purchase, and making you really think about the worth of each dollar. And that is where money mindfulness is king. At starting the thought process, and really starting to understand the role money plays in your life.

Budget 2: Boot camp

The boot camp budget is another great way to NOT budget. Well, not in the traditional sense of the word anyway. You don't need to write any spreadsheets or take too hard a look at your bank accounts (which is a big draw card for people who don't want to know what they spend)! Instead, you pick one thing that you currently buy and cut it out of your life. The money you would normally spend on it becomes your savings.

Here's how the process works:

Take coffee, for example. If you normally buy 3 coffees a day at $4 a pop and cut them out entirely, you could save $84 a week or $4,368 a year. Thought you couldn't afford that overseas holiday? Think again! The boot camp budget is so simple. All it takes is the strength to cut something out of your life that you normally pay for, just one thing, and to then save that money to finance your goal. Make sure you have a goal in mind and that the money you save actually gets put aside.

Take a look at the table below. It shows a savings amount of $3155. And that is for giving up simple things, infrequently, over a year. And I haven't even penciled in all the weeks! Imagine how much more you could save if you cut something every week!

BOOT CAMP BUDGET

Savings goal:	Goal cost:	Goal timeframe:

Item to cut	Cost of item	Time cut for	Amount saved	Total Savings
Coffee	$84 per week	8 weeks	$672	$672
Friday night takeaway	$23 per week	6 weeks	$138	$810
Netflix	$15 per month	3 months	$45	$855
Bootcamp	$50 per week	4 weeks	$200	$1055
Spending money	$100 per week	Once a month	$1200	$2255
Night out	$200	Once a quarter	$800	$3055
Junk from groceries	$20 per week	5 weeks	$100	$3155

The longer you cut something out for, the more money you get. If you decide you can permanently live without the item you cut, then that's great. If not, add it back in and try cutting something else for a while. Perhaps your weekend lunch out, or the little extras you buy at the supermarket (everyone knows they don't count as spending because they're groceries, right? Or maybe that's just me…)

If you really want to test your limits, you can even try cutting multiple things at once. I suggest starting with one thing first though, and building on it later if you want to. Print a graph[35] to fill in for a quick and easy starting point.

[35] http://www.how2without.com/bonus-materials/bbdd-pdf-workbook/

Pros:

- You don't have to spend time setting up a budget or going over it every week.
- You don't have to look too closely at what you spend your money on.
- You can change the expense you cut as often as you like. This means as soon as you get bored or find yourself adding that thing back in, you can swap it for something else.
- It is very easy to succeed at this non-budget for the simple fact that it doesn't take much time or effort.
- You can achieve a surprising amount of savings in a short space of time.

Cons:

- You don't get a firm grasp of where your money is going because you're not budgeting in the true sense of the word.
- You have to actually stick at cutting out the item you choose, which can take a surprising amount of willpower some days.
- You don't learn good financial habits.
- Because you now have savings that you didn't have before, they can end up being used as an emergency fund or a credit card payment system, which swiftly lessens your desire to continue working for it.

Tips and tricks:

Just like being at boot camp, this budget works much better if you have someone egging you on, or holding you accountable. Find a friend who wants to do it with you or announce your plan on social media. Nothing like 100 friends keeping tabs on you!

Once you have decided what you are going to cut, work out how much of a savings this will be every week, and set up an automatic transfer of this amount into a savings account. This ensures that the money gets saved instead of being sucked into your spending.

Attributes for Boot Camp Budget

1- BUDGET TYPE			
My budget should have	Pictures & Graphs	Figures & Facts	Both
My budget should be	Colour	Black and White	Both
This budget is for	Just me	My family	Other
I like budgets that are	Traditional	Non-traditional	New
I want a budget that's	Simple	Neutral	Complex
I want my budget to focus on	Goals	Savings	Making ends meet
I want a budget that is	Flexible	Itemized	Categorized

2- TIME AND COST			
Time a week I can spend on my budget	10 minutes	Under an hour	Under two hours
I want a one off setup time	As short as possible	Under an hour	Anything
I want a budget that costs	Nothing	One-time fee	Ongoing cost

3- KNOWLEDGE			
My math level/tolerance	I hate math	I don't mind math	I'm a math guru
I understand how to use a budget	Not at all	Basic knowledge	In-depth knowledge
I want to know where my money goes	Not at all	Neutral	Definitely
I want to budget	Not at all	Somewhat	Definitely

4- FUTURE PLANNING			
I am saving for	Retirement	Investing	Goals
I want a budget for	Short term	Long term	Don't know
I have these types of debt	Car loan	Student loan	Other debt
I have these types of debt	Credit card	Layby/hire purchase	Personal loan

5- TECHNOLOGY			
Technology and I are	Enemies	Acquaintances	Friends
I want to do my budget	On paper	On the computer	On my phone
I want to sync my budget to	Other tech items	Social media	Nothing!

6- SPENDING HABITS			
When I spend money I use	Mostly cash	Mostly card	Both
When I spend money it's	Spontaneous	Planned	Both
When I see something I really want I	Can walk away	Have to buy it	Different each day
At the end of the week I	Have money left	Am always broke	Different each week

Budget 3: Stick it to yourself

Similar but opposite to the boot camp budget, is the Stick It to Yourself budget. It is still goal based, but instead of having the reward of achieving goals, you give yourself a financial penalty for not sticking to them. If you are the kind of person who is more motivated by risk than reward, then try your hand at this. It is a quick, simple way to achieve goals and prove to others you can stick it to yourself!

Here's how the process works:

Say you want to save $1000 in a 3-month period. Instead, you splurge on a weekend away and miss your goal by a fair proportion. You normally have $100 a week for spending. Because you missed your goal, you now have to forfeit half of that spending money each week until your target is reached.

This is just one example of a penalty. You might decide you have to give up coffee for a week, say no to that new dress you wanted, or work an extra shift. The penalty is up to you. You just need to make sure whatever you choose is enough of an incentive to make you reach for those goals.

It's up to you if you want to do the 10 step budgeting process or not. I personally recommend it, as you will never have a better idea of what you spend your money on than after you've spent time doing those 10 steps. If you can't be bothered though (fair enough), then you just need to make sure your savings goal is an achievable one or you'll always be paying penalties!

1. Work out what your savings target or goal is.

2. Set a date for when you want to achieve that goal.

3. Set a penalty - a hefty one - if you don't complete the goal.

4. Tell everyone about it - make yourself accountable.

5. Stick to it and follow through with the penalty if you fail!

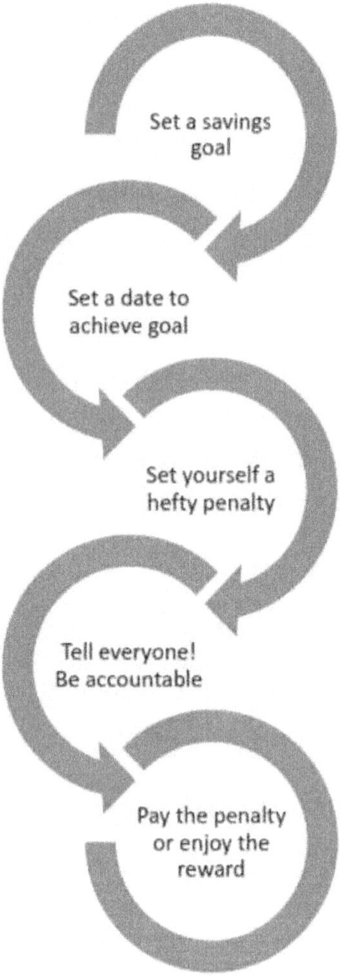

Pros:

- If you need something harsh to motivate you, then this can work really well.
- You don't need to actually 'budget' in the traditional sense of the word.

- It is really simple to set up and follow, and doesn't take much time, either.

Cons:

- This type of budget can be depressing as it is less about reward and more about punishment. I don't know about you, but I do better with rewards.
- If you don't follow through on the penalty, the whole budget falls apart, so you need to ask yourself - how likely are you to follow through?
- Sometimes the reason for your failure is way more enticing than the risk of the penalty. I would really need to make that penalty count to trump a weekend filled with lime milkshakes, sleep-ins, and nightlife. That might just be me though…

Tips and Tricks:

Set an alert on your phone that reminds you how much time you have left to complete your challenge. Tell people what you're up to! If you have all your Facebook friends keeping tabs on your progress, not only will you feel more motivated, but if you don't succeed you are more likely to follow through on your penalty. Create a visual reminder somewhere in your home to remind you to stick at it. You can also attach post-it notes to your credit and debit cards.

Attributes for Stick it to Yourself Budget

1- BUDGET TYPE			
My budget should have	Pictures & Graphs	Figures & Facts	Both
My budget should be	Colour	Black and White	Both
This budget is for	Just me	My family	Other
I like budgets that are	Traditional	Non-traditional	New
I want a budget that's	Simple	Neutral	Complex
I want my budget to focus on	Goals	Savings	Making ends meet
I want a budget that is	Flexible	Itemized	Categorized

2- TIME AND COST			
Time a week I can spend on my budget	10 minutes	Under an hour	Under two hours
I want a one off setup time	As short as possible	Under an hour	Anything
I want a budget that costs	Nothing	One-time fee	Ongoing cost

3- KNOWLEDGE			
My math level/tolerance	I hate math	I don't mind math	I'm a math guru
I understand how to use a budget	Not at all	Basic knowledge	In-depth knowledge
I want to know where my money goes	Not at all	Neutral	Definitely
I want to budget	Not at all	Somewhat	Definitely

4- FUTURE PLANNING			
I am saving for	Retirement	Investing	Goals
I want a budget for	Short term	Long term	Don't know
I have these types of debt	Car loan	Student loan	Other debt
I have these types of debt	Credit card	Layby/hire purchase	Personal loan

5- TECHNOLOGY			
Technology and I are	Enemies	Acquaintances	Friends
I want to do my budget	On paper	On the computer	On my phone
I want to sync my budget to	Other tech items	Social media	Nothing!

6- SPENDING HABITS			
When I spend money I use	Mostly cash	Mostly card	Both
When I spend money it's	Spontaneous	Planned	Both
When I see something I really want I	Can walk away	Have to buy it	Different each day
At the end of the week I	Have money left	Am always broke	Different each week

Recap:

- Money mindfulness: Is a powerful tool to help you better understand your spending, and encourage you to think, act, and benefit from that awareness.
- Boot camp budget: Helps you achieve savings goals, by cutting out items from your spending for periods of time.
- Stick it to yourself budget: Uses financial penalties to motivate you into sticking to your goals.

So what did you think? Are you more of a traditional budget, budget app, or non-budget person? If you can't decide, don't worry. *Chapter 13: What's Your Type? Which Budget Suits You Best?* will help you get everything ironed out. And it's fun, too. Bonus!

CHAPTER 13:
WHAT'S YOUR TYPE? WHICH BUDGET SUITS YOU BEST?

Okay - now the fun part! I've walked you through why you need a budget, what they do, why they often don't work, and how goals and apps can help. We've also looked at all the different types of budgets, including a few non-budgets!

If you haven't found a budget that you think will fit you to a T in the last few chapters, then don't worry. I'm going to help you figure out which budget is your perfect match by looking at your needs and wants, and cross-referencing them with all the budgets.

This chapter is purely optional, so if you already have a budget in mind that you think will work, and you'd like to give it a shot, then skip ahead to *Chapter 14.*

While all budgets have the same goal: getting control of your money, they are not all created equal. Some will work for you, and others won't, it's as simple as that. The aim of this chapter is to find a budget that works with your wants, needs and personality, to create something lasting and easy to use.

You can either fill out the *what's your type* form, compare it to the budgets attributes throughout the book, and then choose a budget you think will be the best fit; or you can take it one step further and add your brain and personality traits into the equation.

We'll go through it step by step, but don't stress, you're going to get a lot of help figuring it out!

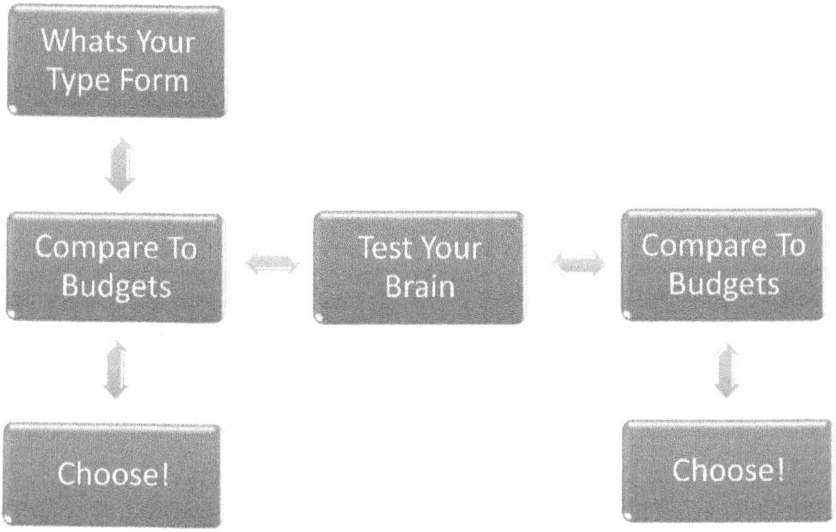

STEP 1

Take a look at the *What's Your Type* form below and either print out a copy[36], or use a piece of paper and pen to draw up your own.

The checklist details all the things that are important to you in a budget, and the spending habits you currently have. Tick one box in each row: Either yes, no, or maybe.

To help you understand what each section of the checklists are talking about, I've defined them below the picture. This will ensure you tick the things that are important to you, and ultimately make sure you end up with the best budget for you personally - not for Fred and Marge down the road.

36 http://www.how2without.com/bonus-materials/bbdd-pdf-workbook/

WHATS YOUR TYPE?

1- BUDGET TYPE			
My budget should have	Pictures & Graphs	Figures & Facts	Both
My budget should be	Colour	Black and White	Both
This budget is for	Just me	My family	Other
I like budgets that are	Traditional	Non-traditional	New
I want a budget that's	Simple	Neutral	Complex
I want my budget to focus on	Goals	Savings	Making ends meet
I want a budget that is	Flexible	Itemized	Categorized

2- TIME AND COST			
Time a week I can spend on my budget	10 minutes	Under an hour	Under two hours
I want a one off setup time	As short as possible	Under an hour	Anything
I want a budget that costs	Nothing	One-time fee	Ongoing cost

3- KNOWLEDGE			
My math level/tolerance	I hate math	I don't mind math	I'm a math guru
I understand how to use a budget	Not at all	Basic knowledge	In-depth knowledge
I want to know where my money goes	Not at all	Neutral	Definitely
I want to budget	Not at all	Somewhat	Definitely

4- FUTURE PLANNING			
I am saving for	Retirement	Investing	Goals
I want a budget for	Short term	Long term	Don't know
I have these types of debt	Car loan	Student loan	Other debt
I have these types of debt	Credit card	Layby/hire purchase	Personal loan

5- TECHNOLOGY			
Technology and I are	Enemies	Acquaintances	Friends
I want to do my budget	On paper	On the computer	On my phone
I want to sync my budget to	Other tech items	Social media	Nothing!

6- SPENDING HABITS			
When I spend money I use	Mostly cash	Mostly card	Both
When I spend money it's	Spontaneous	Planned	Both
When I see something I really want I	Can walk away	Have to buy it	Different each day
At the end of the week I	Have money left	Am always broke	Different each week

Visuals: Do you like to see bright colours and 3D representations of your money and goals? Or do you love your figures and like to see what your money is doing down to the last cent?

Multiple budgets: Do you need to run a personal budget and a family one? Are you hoping to get your partner involved and sync budgets, or is it just for you?

Budget type: Helps you pinpoint what type of budget you like. How much detail would you like your budgets to have? Would you like every item you spend money on to have its own $ amount, or would you just like to sort everything into categories and allocate a lump sum to it? Do you like the fact that traditional budgets are tried, true, and tested? Would you like to try something different?

Cost: Do you want your budget to be free, or are you happy to pay a one-time or a monthly fee? Some of the budgeting apps also have some sections free and some paid, so work out how much you want to spend (if anything), before you download it.

Setup time: This is for that very first time you start your budget, and are setting it up to work for you. It includes downloading programs, syncing to bank accounts or entering details manually, and creating goals and visual aids to help you stick to your budget.

Ongoing time: How much time do you want to spend on your budget every week? Is it something you would like to see just roll along with little or no input from you, or is it something you will enjoy spending a bit of time on? I like to see what's happening with my money and like to feel involved, but I don't want to spend hours on it. You?

Do you hate budgeting and not want to do it at all? How goal oriented do you want your budget? Should it only be about reaching goals, combine goals and finance, or be strictly finance related? Are you still reading this or has your head exploded?

Term of budget: Do you want to budget to achieve a short-term goal, or do you want to get a handle on your money now and into the future?

Math: Do you struggle with math and figures, or just want someone else to do all the work? Do you want to be involved but not constantly adding, or do you love the thought process involved in working out your totals and doing it all yourself?

Knowledge: Do you want to know what you do with your money every week? I mean, really. Do you actually want to know? And are you prepared to make that knowledge work for you?

Savings/Investments/Retirement planning: Do you want to include planning for your retirement within your budget? Do you currently have investments that need managing, or would you like to begin investing? Do you want to save money, either for a small or large goal?

Debt: Do you have debt in the form of credit cards, student loans, personal loans, or car loans? Do you have a mortgage or any form of finance deal that you need your budget to take into consideration, and help you pay off?

Technology: Do you want to sync your computer, tablet, or phone to your budget? Do you want to automate everything and link to all your bank accounts? Or would you prefer to work offline altogether and just use paper and pen? Do you want to be more accountable for your goals and share your excitement and success on social media? Or would you rather just do your own thing without everyone else being in on it?

Spending habits: Do you normally spend your money with cash, card, or a mixture of both? Do you plan what you spend your money on, or do you find things you love and just buy them? Can you desperately want something and just walk away, or do you have to buy it? Do you spend more than you make every week, and struggle to pay off the backlog, or do you have money left over?

* * *

Following these steps, and picking out a personal budget, is far more important than you think. I know, I know, people have been doing spreadsheet budgets for years. But how many of those people *still* budget?

While following the crowd and picking something everyone else does may work for some, for many it becomes just another thing they failed out. Not only is this terrible for self-esteem, budgeting then becomes 'that hard thing I couldn't do.'

STEP 2

Once you've completed the *What's Your Type* form, go through the book and compare it to the attributes for each budget. These are found at the end of each budgets tips and tricks. The different budget types highlighted will support varying aspects of budgeting (or not budgeting) that work best with you, and your life.

Find the two budgets that fit best with what you have highlighted on the *What's Your Type* form. If you're confident that one of those budgets will work for you then skip ahead to step 5.

STEP 3

How you learn, and process information, plays a large role in how well implementing something new will work out for you. If you are an incredibly creative person who learns visually and with images and patterns, then an analytically based spreadsheet just isn't going to cut the mustard.

If you haven't already, take an online quiz that shows you how you learn,[37] and which side of your brain is more dominant.[38] These will give you another angle from which to assess a budget.

There is new research which suggests learning styles and right/left brain patterns are something that can be taught as well, not just something you are born with, which is controversial but interesting.

However, as we are trying to assess how you learn and interact right *now*, I believe these tests will still be incredibly helpful in choosing your ultimate budget. You can simply Google 'Learning Styles Test' and 'Brain Dominance Test' or use my links to a couple of tests I found.

STEP 4

The graph below loosely shows which budgets fit right and left brain preferences, and learning types. The budgets at the bottom can be used with any learning style. Cross-reference your test results from step 3 with the different budgets and apps, and see which ones are the best fit. Choose the 2 budgets that you think fit your learning types and brain the best.

[37] http://www.learning-styles-online.com/inventory/questions.php?cookieset=y

[38] http://www.queendom.com/tests/access_page/index.htm?idRegTest=3181

BUDGETS THAT MATCH YOUR BRAIN AND LEARNING STYLES

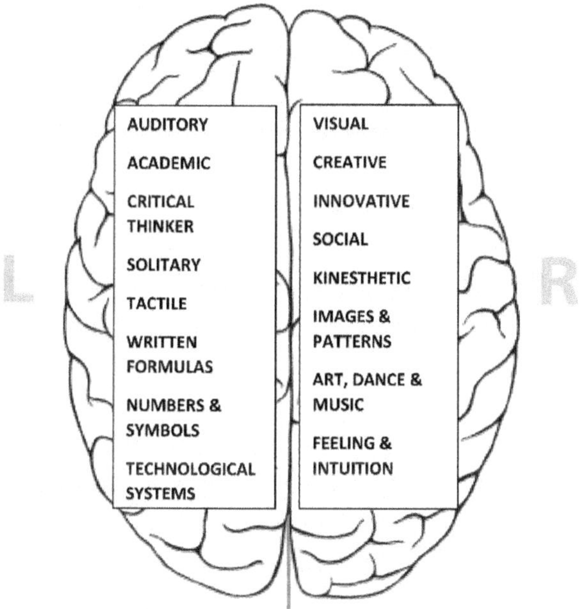

SPREADSHEET BUDGET
CATEGORY/ENVELOPE BUDGET
CASHLESS BUDGET
PERCENTAGE BUDGET

BUDGETING APPS
CASH BASED BUDGET
MINDFULNESS
BOOT CAMP BUDGET

SPEND AND SAVE BUDGET
BUCKET LIST BUDGET
STICK IT TO YOURSELF BUDGET
3 STEP BUDGET
CHOOSE YOUR OWN ADVENTURE

STEP 5

So now you should have two or four budget choices from the completed graph/s. One showing you the two budgets that most closely match your needs, and (if you did steps 3 and 4) one showing the two budgets that most closely match your learning styles. I want you to look at these four budgets together now and find the common ground.

If you've got 2 budgets the same then that's you're winner. Of course it's not generally that easy, so if you're having trouble picking the best one out of your four budgets, then think about the one that you were first drawn to.

We tend to be pulled towards the things that appeal and work for us, so you shouldn't have any problems finding a match. Another way is to look for the similarities in the four budgets and pick the one that has the most connections to the other three.

If you're struggling, go back and check your list of needs, and make sure they are accurate. If you want to try all four budgets - do! Just make sure you give them all a fair go before you swap. The more you muck around with your budget, the longer it will take to see change.

If the perfect budget still isn't obvious, then don't panic! Remember the 'Choose Your Own Adventure' budget? It helps you combine multiple budgets to suit all of your needs.

It is much easier, however, to find one budget that has a good fit, especially when starting out, than to try and juggle multiple budgeting aspects. So do try to give something a go. You can always reassess things later on.

Recap:

- Picking a budget that suits you and your needs is very important.
- How you learn and process information plays a big part in choosing a budget.
- Finding the right budget does not have to be hard. Just go through the steps to compare the budgets, and find your perfect match.
- Stick with the budget you choose long enough to be certain it is or isn't working. If it doesn't, try again. You might not get it right first time around.

That's it! You've downloaded your worksheets[39] and picked the budget that will work best for you and your life. But what do you do with it?

Never fear - all your questions will be answered up next in *Chapter 14: I've Got a Budget. Now What?* We'll also go over some of the best tips and tricks for sticking to a budget and realising your dreams.

---

[39] http://www.how2without.com/bonus-materials/bbdd-pdf-workbook/

CHAPTER 14:
I'VE GOT A BUDGET. NOW WHAT?

You've finally got yourself an awesome budget. One that works with your life, the way you learn and think, and will help you reach your goals. But now what? What do you do with this incredible budget?

The planning stage of anything new is always the bit I find the most exciting, and I know this is true for many people. Actually implementing your new plan is trickier, and way more boring. If you have been taking the book one step at a time, and doing the tasks, then you should have:

1. Worked out what you actually spend over 4 weeks, using our 10-step process in *Chapter 3*

2. Completed the *Wants and Needs* checklist. (optional)

3. Completed a brain and personality test online (optional)

4. Found the budget/s that most closely match your needs and personality

If you haven't done all of these things and don't have your weekly spend and perfect budget in hand, then go back and get it sorted. There is no point trying to make a budget work if you haven't found one that suits you. Once you're sorted, follow these steps:

Set your budget up: Set aside some time in your crazy life to set up your budget and get it working the way you want it to. This should only be a one-time effort, so make sure you give yourself an ample amount of time to get it set up well, first time. This should include downloading or printing off anything you need, setting up bank accounts, categories, or items, and setting specific short- and long-term goals.

Allocate time: Next, allocate some time each week, or month, to work on your budget. This doesn't have to be much. It might be 30 minutes on your phone on the way to work, or an hour one evening. Use this time to see how everything is flowing, track your goals, and make changes where needed. Make sure you do this consistently. If you are not actively involved in your budget, it will become just another one of those things that you started and never continued. Like Zumba...

Be excited and inspired! The goals you set up when you wrote and implemented your budget should make you want to start tap dancing or break into song. If they don't, then there is something seriously wrong, and you need to rethink them. Life was not meant to be boring. It was meant to be lived!

If your goals don't excite you, then why would you want to put the effort into making them happen? That's right - you wouldn't. So get excited! Share your goals with someone. Become accountable. Post them on social media along with a date, or make yourself a poster, or a picture board, to remind yourself just what you're aiming for.

Evolve. Don't let your budget stagnate. Lives change, and your budget needs to change too. If you start earning more income, or buy a membership for your local gym, add it to your budget. Your budget is only as accurate as you make it.

Make sure if you reach a goal to add another one or two to your ladder. The moment you stop reaching for the next rung is the moment you get stuck. Always look for more in life. Whatever it is, it's out there, waiting for you to grab it with both hands. But it's not going to come to you.

Persevere. A good budget - hopefully the one you now have - is there to support your life, not rule it! And like any support, it's not always going to be perfect. Expect to have days where it feels more like a restraint than a support. Plan for days that you fail - because you will. A one-day, or even a one-week fail, does not mean the end of the line. It just means you're human. Get back into it and give it another shot!

Not everything succeeds right away. Not even the perfect budget. Budgeting is something you build on, month after month and year after year. The longer you stick at it, the better it will become. Here are a few things you can do though, if you're finding the going hard:

- Accept it probably is! Budgeting may not be something you're used to, and anything new takes time and patience. Don't give up just because it's tricky. Soon budgeting will become second nature and super easy!

- Reassess your budget, and make sure you have allocated enough 'free' money to continue enjoying life. (We'll talk more about this in Book 2 of our *$mall Change - Big Reward$* series, where we tackle spending and saving).

- Revisit your budgeting 'needs' and make sure the things that are important to you are covered. If they're not, re-do your checklist and pick a more appropriate budget. Make sure you've given a budget a really good shot before swapping.

- Focus on the goals you're going to reach, not the path you're taking to get there. Reaching your dreams is a huge confidence lift and will help you see budgeting as a positive instead of a negative.

No-one can make you budget, any more than they can make you diet, but *Brilliant Budgets and Despicable Debt* should have helped you work out and set up your perfect budget, and made budgeting more accessible. It should also have given you a solid understanding of why budgeting is important, and how to implement and succeed at one. It's up to you now to make sure it works.

Recap:

- Make sure you have your expenses worked out, and your perfect budget picked, before trying to implement anything.
- Set your budget up and allocate regular times to review it.
- Be excited about your goals - they will help your budget succeed where it would otherwise fail.
- Make sure your budget changes with you and your life.
- Stick at it! Nothing comes easily, and the rewards far outweigh the negatives.

Hopefully by now you know the how, the why, and the different types of budgeting. You should have worked out your ultimate budget, and set it up with everything you need to make it work for you. Check out *Chapter 15 - Tips and Tricks: The Keys to Success* for any extra help you may need.

CHAPTER 15:

TIPS AND TRICKS: THE KEYS TO SUCCESS

With any budget, the key to making it through, really sticking to it, and seeing great results is finding little things that make the budget easier for you. These will be different for every person. And things that worked for you in the past may not work again! So if you get stuck, are finding the going tough, or just need an extra boost, refer back to this chapter for some great tips and tricks.

It's also a great place to start if you need some inspiration for tackling debt. Sometimes it can take a while for that Despicable Debt to disappear and small things can make a big difference!

Starting out

Make sure you have read through the book and completed all the steps listed. These aren't just there as filler - you need each and every one of them for your budget to have the best chance of success. All the checklists, forms and examples to help you with this are available for free on our website.[40]

1. Write down why you wanted to start budgeting. Refer back to this throughout your journey so you don't lose track of why you're doing it.

2. Only you know what you spend your money on. Make sure you work out exactly what you spend, and on what, before trying to budget, save, or pay off debt.

[40] http://www.how2without.com/bonus-materials/bbdd-pdf-workbook/

3. Get rid of your excuses. We dealt with them all in *Chapter 2*, and they have no place in your mind.

4. Overcome your fears. Budgeting done right makes life easier, not harder. So whether it's fear of change, of rejection, of ridicule, or of failure, set it aside and push on. You will be stronger for it at the other end.

5. You may not get your budget right the first time - and that's okay. Just try again. The longer you do it, the easier it becomes.

6. Complete the checklists and graphs I've included in the workbook[41], as these will give you an instant idea of what components are going to work best for you. Don't just pick a budget at random, or because a friend recommended it. Find one that suits how you and your life are today, as of this moment. Budgets that suited you 5 years ago may not now.

7. Give the budget you choose a chance to work, before swapping it out for something new.

8. Create short-term and long-term goals. Short-term goals help you stay motivated for long periods of time and encourage you to stick to your budget. Long-term goals are a marker of your success, and something to look forward to. Both will help you succeed where other things fail.

9. Create a picture board as a visual reminder of your goal, or write a list and hang it where you will see it often.

10. Look for the joy in your goals, no matter how outwardly boring, and get excited!

---

41 http://www.how2without.com/bonus-materials/bbdd-pdf-workbook/

11. If it feels restrictive then it is not a good fit. You should always have money for spending on things you want, just for the sake of wanting them - even if you're trying to pay off debt.

12. Create a chart showing how your budget will influence and help every area of your life. If your budget isn't meeting all your needs, then you will need to alter it, or find a new one that does.

13. Make time every week to track your finances. The more involved you are, the better you will understand your budget, your habits, and your money. Understanding your finances gives you the power and the ability to grow, change, and succeed!

14. If you struggle with visualizing how much all the little expenses make a difference in your finances, then create or print[42] a pie chart of your spending money. Add up all the money you spend on coffee, eating out, entertainment, and shopping, etc., and allocate them their own 'pie' segments. I guarantee it will be a real eye opener!

Sticking with it

1. Attach post-it notes to your credit and debit cards, reminding you of your goals or telling you not to spend money.

2. Make your cash and cards hard to access, so it reminds you to think about your spending.

3. Look at all your direct debits and ongoing memberships and see if you can cut or minimize any of them.

---

[42] http://www.how2without.com/bonus-materials/bbdd-pdf-workbook/

4. Review your budget from time to time to make sure it is still working for you.

5. Make sure you give any budget you start a decent shot. It will take time to know if it is working or not.

6. Budgeting requires a willingness to change. If you're thinking about the money you're spending, but never converting those thoughts to actions, then nothing will work. Make sure you follow through.

7. Find a friend or a family member who will hold you accountable with your goals, encourage you, and drag you back into line if you stray.

8. Announce your goals, along with a date, on social media. Keep people in the loop by updating how you're going. The more people who know about your goals, the less likely you are to give up.

9. Set up your savings account in a separate bank, without Internet banking or a debit/credit card. This way you can only withdraw your money if you make the effort to go to the bank. No late night shopping slips!

10. Buy a lockup or tie up wallet as a way of reminding you to think about your spending.

11. If you are going shopping, tell an accompanying friend to remind you of your goals before each purchase. Set alarms on your phone telling you to think before you spend. Give yourself a monetary limit and withdraw it in cash, don't take your credit card! Write on your hand if you have to!

12. Set up a separate account to store your bill money in. This way, it will roll over each week until needed, without being frittered away.

13. Buy a wallet that separates your cash into categories, with the ability to label each section as you like.

14. Stash emergency money away for each category or as a lump sum. This means if you spend too much, you have backup until payday rolls around again, without having to break into your savings, even if it means you can only afford 'emergency items.'

15. Load money onto fuel or transport cards so you never have to take a credit card with you for 'emergencies.'

16. Instead of having a credit card for emergencies, take a debit card, which has a finite amount of cash on it - but still only use it for emergencies.

17. Set up a direct debit with your savings amount each week, so you don't even have to think about it.

18. Encourage friends to complete your goals with you. Find a common goal and help each other stay on target.

19. Give yourself a baseline of what you can spend on a card. For example: you can't use your card for any purchase under $50. This stops the little expenditures that add up every week and become large amounts!

20. Set yourself a credit card-free goal and see how long you can last. You'd be amazed how much you might save.

21. If you can't get used to only spending cash, but don't want to use your credit card, then load your spending money onto a debit card each week and use that instead.

22. Set up an app or an alert on your phone that reminds you how much time you have left to complete your goal. The more you think about your money in relation to goals, the easier it becomes not to spend it.

23. If you know you will always fall back on your credit cards - cut them up! And if you can't bring yourself to do that, give them to a friend or family member with instructions to only return them for medical emergencies or similar.

24. If you are always on the go and finding time for finances is hard, then look into the apps. Apps can save time by sorting through your finances in a fraction of the time you could. If you're short on time and find an app you trust with your bank details, then make use of it. Why struggle if you don't have to? Apps allow you to keep track of your money and your goals, on your smartphone, wherever you are!

25. If an app is accessing your bank accounts, make sure it has a secure encryption, and excellent reviews and security settings. Also add a password and antivirus software to your phone.

26. It is better to save less over a longer period, than to save more for a short period and then give up. Make sure you are saving at a sustainable level.

These are some of the tips and tricks that have worked for me, and for people I have spoken with, over the years. If you have any that have worked for you, I would love to hear them! Join the conversation on Facebook[43] or on Twitter[44], and share the love.

---

[43] https://www.facebook.com/how2without/

[44] http://www.twitter.com/heidi2233/

That's all, folks! End of the line. Check out the *Conclusion* for a wrap up of *Brilliant Budgets and Despicable Debt.*

CONCLUSION

The word budget once used to mean "pouch" or "purse." A budget, therefore, is literally "what's in the pouch."

Translation: It's not about how much you earn, it's not even about what method you use to budget. It's about how much is left in the pouch at the end of the day. It's what you can hold onto. That is, and always will be, what counts.

And that has been the sole aim of this book: to provide you with as many different ways of budgeting and holding onto your money as possible, in the hopes that one of them will work for you. Because if you can't hold onto any of your money now, then how will you manage it in the future? Short answer - you won't. Your future will end up managing you.

There is no reason for not budgeting, for staying out of debt, or managing your money on some level. We've covered all the excuses and all the genuine problems people face when budgeting, and found solutions to the lot. Yes, it can take time, and yes, it can be a learning curve. The more complex the budget, the steeper the curve. But just like anything else worthwhile, the results drastically outweigh any problems you may face.

Budgeting is something you have to be willing to give a good shot. There's no point trying 10 different budgets in a month and declaring them all a failure because you want to go back to your blissful ignorance. Give them a decent shot and you'll be amazed at how they can change your life.

Debt too is something that needs to be worked on over time. Changing the habits of a lifetime is not easy, and will often take a bit of trial and error before you get it right. But man is it worth it in the long run!

People constantly ask me how I can afford to travel, or go on adventures with my family. The answer is simple. I decide on what I want, I plan how I can achieve it, and I set out to make it happen. And it's never as hard as you think it is. Yes, I give up some things I like, in order to do others I love. I go without now, so I can have more at a later date. But the end always justifies the means.

I have never reached a goal I set and said, 'Well, that wasn't worth it!' I see staying out of debt through mindfulness and budgeting as a way to enhance life, to rise above the everyday and achieve the things we have previously only dreamed about. And you can!

If I had to condense this whole book into one line, it would be:

Keep it simple. Set goals. Save hard. Succeed.

That is the basis of a good budget. It doesn't have to be hard or complex. It doesn't have to be time consuming or data heavy. It just has to work for you, and with you. I sincerely hope that this book has helped you better understand how to tackle your finances, pay off debt, and achieve the goals you want; now, and in the future.

I'd say good luck, but I believe you make your own luck! So, I'll leave you with this instead.

Plan, to succeed!

BONUS MATERIALS

There is an entire workbook that complements *Brilliant Budgets and Despicable Debt;* Book 1 in our *$mall Change - Big Reward$* series. You can download and print[45] it any time you like. This will help you implement everything we've covered throughout the book and achieve your goals faster and with less hassle.

Budgeting and overcoming debt are the first steps towards financial success, but keep an eye out for the rest of the *$mall Change - Big Reward$* series, which will cover: saving, spending, investing, and retiring.

---

[45] http://www.how2without.com/bonus-materials/bbdd-pdf-workbook/

PLEASE REVIEW THIS BOOK

Reviews are like food to hungry authors!

I love reading reviews and I know other people do too. If you liked this book (or hated it) please leave a constructive review so I can improve as an author and other readers can make informed decisions.

I sincerely hope you found loads of useful information in *Brilliant Budgets and Despicable Debt.*

Look out for more *$mall Change – Big Reward$* books in the near future, and don't forget to join our readers list[46] so you're first in line for our new books

Review this book now, and let people know what you thought.

[46] http://www.how2without.com/home/join-our-team/get-free-books/

ACKNOWLEDGEMENTS

Special thanks to my Mum, for teaching me how to budget early on, a skill that has been invaluable throughout my life.

To Clinton for always finding ways to do what we love, without spending a fortune - thank you! You make it so much easier to stick to a budget with your eternal optimism and love of the outdoors.

To Molly, you remind me what I'm working towards, and it is so gratifying seeing you learn to save, to spend wisely (most of the time - I'll never forget the pink octopus!) and enjoy everything in life, regardless of the price.

To Matthew and Vanessa, thank you for your late night tech support, and for always making time for me when I know it's in short supply.

To my amazing editor Elaine who always adds such value to my work, and to Angie Mroczka for her tech support at random times, first edition cover, and unending patience. You're amazing!

To all my wonderful Authorpreneur friends - you guys rock! I could always count on you for knowledge, encouragement and support.

And finally to all my fans, who provided feedback and reviews and made my book the success it is today - thank you, from the bottom of my heart.

ABOUT THE AUTHOR

Heidi lives in sunny Sydney with her husband, daughter, and dog Gonzo, where she likes to swim, rock climb, and sew. She grew up in beautiful New Zealand, famous for 'kiwi ingenuity' — and of course rugby, and also spent 2 1/2 years living in and wandering around England and Europe. She loves hanging out with family, travelling, tasting new foods, and exploring everything life has to offer.

She doesn't believe in missing out just because you have a bit less in your pocket either! Growing up, her family was not well off and as she got older she was terrible with money. Over the years she has learnt to adapt to what life throws at her, and be savvy with her money. This life-long battle has morphed into an understanding and knowledge of money and finance as a whole that she doesn't think people who grow up with a bit more are able to replicate.

She has been writing for many years, and this is her second nonfiction finance book. *Mortgage Free* was an instant bestseller and *Brilliant Budgets and Despicable Debt* is the first of 3 books in her new *$mall Change – Big Reward$* series.

Lightning Source UK Ltd.
Milton Keynes UK
UKOW05n1440181016

285574UK00001B/20/P

9 780994 517142